Nanny Basics

and Beyond

Nanny Basics

and Beyond

Marcia Hall

What people are saying about

Nanny Basics and Beyond

"Marcia Hall has done something truly amazing with this book. Not only has she given freely of her thoughtful and meaningful insights into being a nanny, she has gathered an 'A list' of nanny industry superstars to share their information as well. You can get the combined knowledge of the true pioneers of the industry as they share practical advice on being a nanny. *Nanny Basics and Beyond* can be a guide for those just starting out, a reminder for those a few years in, and an inspiration for all nannies." Sue Downey, owner Nannypalooza and interNational Nanny Training Day

"As a nanny mentor and educator, I recommend several resources to my mentees. *Nanny Basics and Beyond* is definitely my 'go to' book for all things Nanny A to Z." Angela Johnson, Ask the Nanny; https://www.facebook.com/ askthenanny

"*Nanny Basics and Beyond* is definitely a must-read for every professional nanny or for anyone hoping to start a career as a nanny. I'm simply thrilled that Marcia has taken her wealth of knowledge and shared it with us. When she writes that 'You can spend 40 years in the nanny industry and still not fully understand the intricacies of the job,' that statement is an incredible truth. Every nanny needs to pick up a copy of this book!" Alene Mathurin, author and founder of My Nanny Circle; MyNannyCircle.com

Dedication:

To dad and mom, who never once thought of me as "just a nanny." From the very beginning you have supported, encouraged, and cheered me on.

Mom, there are not enough words to express how grateful I am to you. You have been an inspiration to me with your patience, service, and love. Thank you for always believing in me.

Dad, even though you now live in heaven, I know you are watching me with pride. I can only hope to continue your legacy of dedication, determination, and sacrifice.

Acknowledgments.

To Becky Kavanagh and Glenda Propst. I am forever grateful to you for the support, encouragement, and hours of assistance to me as I got Nanny Coaching Team off the ground and wrote this book. Simply put, this would not have happened without each of you.

Scott, you are my partner in every sense of the word. This book is as much your accomplishment as it is mine. Thank you for being my ally and advocate. I love everything about this truly crazy life we have built.

To Nadia, Lucy, and Isaac. For the last two years you have shared me with this project. You have sacrificed time with me so I could complete this book and listened to me talk about it endlessly. I owe you a trip to Disney!

To my brother, Gene. Thank you for your continued support and encouragement to finish this project. The many hours of babysitting were not in vain. I could not have completed it without your assistance.

To every individual who I interviewed for this book and through Nanny Coaching Team. You have shared your knowledge with me so I could share it with the world. Please accept my heartfelt gratitude. You have helped to enhance and uplift this industry. You each should be celebrated.

To the current and past INA Board of Directors. I am honored to serve our industry next to each of you. Your hard work and dedication is making a difference.

To my CITC family. For more than 20 years I have worshiped alongside you. You have helped me to mature in my faith and grow in my leadership. Thank you for blessing me with your friendship and love.

Foreword

"The hand that rocks the cradle rules the world." William Ross Wallace

The path you've chosen for your career will have a profound impact on the children you help raise, and on the families with whom you choose to work. Nannies are not babysitters; you've chosen a profession, not just a job.

And? Parents today are not just busy, they are also very worried. Worried that they don't know what they're doing, that their children won't be "OK," that there are too many roadblocks for them to succeed as parents. Even parents who think they are only looking for someone to "watch the kids" are really looking for so much more.

As a parenting and youth development expert, I know intimately the fears that parents face. When you choose a family and integrate yourself into the role of nanny, you'll be not only the person keeping children safe and fed and where they need to be, you'll also be guiding and shaping their journey, answering their 7.2 million questions each day, interpreting the world with them and for them as you spend each moment together. Even more, you'll become a parent coach and mentor. You'll answer parent questions about why a child is or isn't doing something, about what decisions to make, about rules and chores and consequences....

It's a privilege—for sure! It's also really hard, very important work.

All of this gives you just a glimpse into the complexities of finding and choosing the best situation for yourself. In order to do your best for a family, you need to do your best for yourself. Choose the right opportunity, and set up communication, contracting, and conflict resolution (just to name a few) right from the beginning.

Why this book?

In *Nanny Basics and Beyond* you will find a road map. This book is the only one you need to set yourself up for success as a professional nanny. It would be great if such a guide existed for every industry, but that just isn't the case. These pages contain the best advice from a number of the most respected people in the nanny world. You may rely on these experts to care about you, want the best for you, and give you the benefit of everything they have learned in—altogether—hundreds of years of experience!

You will read real-life stories about what went well, and what went badly, for nannies just like you. You will learn from their difficulties and have the advantage of taking their wisdom into every professional conversation from now on. You'll read with a smile as you hear their genuine compassion for the struggles nannies can face—they won't pretend it's all easy—and the joys nannies get to bask in during their time with—and for years after they become part of—a family.

And you will find your inspiration. *Nanny Basics and Beyond* is a compilation of advice that gives you the chance to stand on the shoulders of those who forged a respected industry when many people in our society see it as a "just a job in childcare." This book will help you clarify why this is the right profession for you, and will remind you that you are not alone when you face a challenging work environment. Instead, it will lead you through.

Use this as a guidebook, and not only for your first interview and contract negotiation. There are situations here—like divorced families, families with multiples, facing trauma—that you may not see until you've been working for years. There are moments that don't come with every job—like how to make a teen more resilient, or helping parents with a special-needs child—but often show up in the course of a career. You'll want to keep this book on hand for years to come.

When you choose a profession dedicated to helping children and families, it can seem as if that calling is enough. That the sense of purpose you feel will overcome all obstacles and smooth out all communication. As amazing, as uplifting, as your desire is to help and care...it's not enough to ensure your safety and job security. This book is what you need to make your calling into a career that fulfills while it sustains.

—Dr. Deborah Gilboa, MD

Table of Contents

Introduction

Being a nanny can be the most rewarding job, but can also be one of the most challenging. From finding a balance between discipline and nurturing to working in harmony with parents, there is so much to learn. You can spend 40 years in the nanny industry and still not fully understand all the intricacies of the job.

The relationships you form are unique to this industry. Collaborating with parents who ultimately have the final say in the lives of the children you care for can often cause friction in the home. Finding your place in the family adds to the confusion that nannies see on the job. It is your responsibility to navigate the partnership with grace and understanding.

In my years as a nanny, I have made many mistakes, but I learned from every one of them. This book is my chance to share many of the tips that I have learned along the way. I am also giving you the opportunity to hear from other leaders within the nanny industry as they share their unique insights.

We are a diverse industry, and my goal for this book is that it will speak to each of you. I hope that you nannies who are just starting out in your career and those who have been working in the industry for years can learn and grow through the experience of others.

—Marcia Hall

SECTION I: THE BASICS

Nanny Basics and Beyond

Chapter 1. The Dream versus the Reality

"As a nanny, you can make an impact in the life of children, but it is a continual learning experience."
Glenda Propst

Glenda Propst of Nanny Transitions shared her thoughts on this topic with me. Her 30 years in the industry plus countless experiences coaching and mentoring nannies allow Glenda to understand the difference between the dream nannies have and the reality that they face.

How did you find your way here? Did you enjoy babysitting in your teens so much that you wanted to continue? Did you move into the nanny world from daycare or another school setting? Did you transition here from the nursing or in some other way? Many roads lead to this profession. Regardless of how you got here, I am sure that you have a number of specific expectations for your job.

Your job will likely start in what I like to call the "honeymoon" phase. It can be a marvelous time when you can't wait to start your day. The employer is grateful to you, you are just starting to get to know the children and they are, for the most part, well behaved, and all your expectations are being met. However, the "honeymoon" can be short-lived, and reality can hit you hard while on the job. There are several simple ways to avoid the honeymoon crash.

The process of setting expectations so that both you and your employer can meet those expectations starts with the interview, but continues throughout the job.

The Right Conversations to Have

When a parent interviews for a new child care provider, she asks questions so that she can understand the level of care that you will give to her child. The same is right for you. You should ask thoughtful questions to try to get the parent to reveal what the job will be like on a day-to-day basis.

It is easy to make the mistake of not asking the hard or awkward questions in the interview process, just because these questions can be uncomfortable. You need to remember those questions will become even more challenging to ask later on. When you bring up an issue in the interview, it is just a question. When asking about that topic after the job has started, it becomes a problem and that makes it personal. Requesting a change to an item that you have already agreed to can cause anxiety to you, anger to the parent, and confusion to the children.

There are many conversations that help you gain a better understanding of the family. The most important thing to understand is how the parent sees your role in the family. The answer the parent gives to this question will provide you with insight into her expectations and an understanding of how you will fit into the family. The goal of this question is to figure out if your skills and temperament match the family's needs and personality.

You should also ask about a typical day working in the home. This question will help you understand what you can expect from the job. It will help you understand how well the parent realizes what goes on in her house from day to day. A parent who is hands-off might not have a full understanding of a typical day. A new parent might also not have a good understanding of what a typical day will entail. Having this conversation gives you a chance to spotlight your skills while you explain what a nanny should do in a typical day.

Legal pay is also a topic you should discuss. For a better understanding of what this means, see Chapter 3. This subject should be discussed early in the interview process as it will help determine if you are going to move forward with more interviews. A parent who wants to avoid this question or does not come back with an emphatic "of course I will pay you legally" may not have a good understanding of what a professional nanny is and does. Asking this up front will mean no one is wasting his or her time.

Discussing how long the parent intends to employ a nanny is a meaningful discussion to have. The parents might be looking for a nanny just for a year or two while their baby is young, and others are looking for a long-term commitment. Knowing this ahead of time will help set expectations for the future. While this is a crucial topic, you should also keep in mind that a parent's needs and desires could change. If the parent tells you she only wants a nanny for a year, she may soon see the benefit of having in-home care for her children. She might end up wishing you would stay forever, or she may start out wanting to have long-term care only to find that it does not work for her family.

Discipline and child-rearing philosophies need to be a discussed. This conversation is meant to get to the heart of how to become a partner with the parent. Keep in mind that the parent might adopt more than one philosophy and or not adhere to any particular style of discipline. A new parent may not know to which theory she plans to subscribe. However, it is critical that you have a similar parenting

Chapter 1. The Dream versus the Reality

outlook. If both parties cannot agree on how to steer children in the right direction, then both will be very frustrated. It is essential that you be able to embrace the child-rearing style of the parent or that the parent is willing to embrace yours. Presenting a united front should begin when the child is in infancy but, as the child matures, it becomes a critical part of working together as a team.

Ask the parent how she wants you to handle emergencies. This topic can be telling because, beyond the obvious crises when you would need to call 911, the parent's answer can show how much responsibility she places in your hands. If she wants you to call for every fall and scrape, you will know that this parent will likely want an account for every activity her child engages in, even the small ones. If she tells you that unless it is a critical emergency, she wants to know about it at the end of the day, then it means that she will likely put a lot of trust in your abilities. She will not expect you to notify her for every minor injury at the time that it happens. This will also likely mean that she trusts your judgment about daily activities that you participate in with the children. Of course, even with a parent who does not want to know about every incident, you should document them all for your own protection.

A parent of a baby or young children can often feel sad when she needs to be away from her children for the "firsts" of their lives. You can ask the parent how she would like you to handle it when and if the child rolls over for the first time or says his or her first words. For older children, you might ask if the parent wants to chaperone school field trips or call her if the children have a bad day at school. The answers can help you to understand how sensitive she will be to missing those milestones. These questions also give you insight about how the parent feels about being away and how she feels about having a nanny. It's a reflection of her faith in you and confidence in herself as a parent.

Code Words and Red Flags

It can be easy to get caught up in the emotions of the interview experience, especially when you need a job. While there are code words you can listen for to tell you that something is off, using your instinct will help keep you from families that are just not right. Instincts will help you navigate away from families that are raising red flags.

> "If money becomes an issue in the interview, it will continue to be an issue throughout the position." Glenda Propst

Money is one of the most significant red flags. The parent might not make it obvious, but you should listen to the implications and insinuations as well as out-and-out statements.

Chapter 1. The Dream versus the Reality

If money comes up more than the care of the children, what the expectations of the job are, or what the relationships between you and the parent should look like, then money is likely the parent's primary priority, and it will continue to be.

"Flexibility" is another word you should listen for. Flexibility in and of itself is not a bad thing. Most parents want a nanny who can be flexible around the needs of the family. "Flexibility" used in the job description could mean that the parent needs to change the agreed-upon work schedule often or that she wants you to be able to adjust to the children's activities. It could mean that she wants you to be on call or ready and willing to work at the last minute. While you should want to be flexible when possible, these concessions can often morph into the parent taking advantage of you. You need a better understanding of what the parent means by "flexible," as well as how flexible the parent can be when you need to make adjustments to your schedule.

"Basic cleaning" and "tidying up" are phrases that nannies will hear a lot. The topic of cleaning can be a touchy subject for many nannies. As childcare professionals, you should be proud that you are in the home to focus on the care of the children. While necessary care and cleaning of the children's belongings, toys, clothes, and linen can be inherent with the custody of the children, many times when a parent says to "keep the house tidy," she has a very different idea of what that entails than you do. It is imperative that you get a solid understanding of exactly what the parent will be asking you to do. It is equally important to get it in writing when and if you accept the job.

Salary is a hot button when it comes to wages. Many of the parents who will employ you are professionals who receive a salary rather than hourly rate. A parent may want to pay you in this manner. However, it is important to realize that nannies in the US are not legally able to be paid a "salary." If you hear a parent use this term in an interview, it is best to get clarity on what she means, and it is a good idea for you to go to the interview with a basic understanding of why it is not legal for her to pay you in this way. You will find further details on this topic in Chapter 3.

The Heart of the Job

The environment that the nanny works in is vital to the success of the job. You should have at least one interview in the home where you will be working. As you interview, make a note of the environment and atmosphere. Can you see yourself working in this setting? Is it disorganized, and you worry that you will be regularly cleaning up messes for which you should not be responsible? Is it overly clean and tidy, and you are afraid that creative messes will not be accepted? You need to know your comfort

Chapter 1. The Dream versus the Reality

level when it comes to organization, clutter, and messiness, and work in an environment in which you are comfortable.

The environment is also about the interaction between the children and their parents. You should look around the house for photos and children's art. What stories do they tell? How do the children interact when their parents are present? These all can be an indication of the home environment.

You should also pay attention to the interaction between parents. Partners or spouses who are willing to work together to solve issues will also be more willing to see you as an equal partner in the family. Do they work as a team or does only one of them talk? Do they take turns in the care of the children or does one of them do most of the work? These are details that are inappropriate to ask directly, but, if you can naturally observe the parents, you can see for yourself the dynamic in the family.

To better understand the reality of the job from the parent's perspective, you should ask how she would like you to communicate. Knowing this can help you see how involved in day-to-day activities she wants to be. The process of finding, being offered, and selecting a job can be a good indication of the parent's communication style. If she does not seem to use a lot of technology, but you communicate almost exclusively in this manner, you may end up with a communication problem. The most effective communication happens when both parties use the systems that fit with their personality. If you are not tech savvy, then working for a parent who wants to use the latest technology to communicate is going to be a problem. You should also ask yourself if you are willing to learn new skills for this job or not.

History Dictates Future

One of the best ways to understand the reality of a nanny position is to talk about the family's childcare history. It can be tricky to get honest answers from the parent on this topic. You should ask open-ended questions rather than questions she can answer with a "yes" or "no." For example, instead of asking "Have you had nannies in the past," you could say, "Tell me a little bit about your past child care providers." This invites more dialogue about the topic.

When you are interviewing with a family who has had nannies in the home, it can be eye-opening to know why that nanny left (or is leaving) and hear what kind of relationship the children still have with their previous caregivers. Did the parent let the former nanny go without warning? Was there an urgent reason to do this? Did she allow the children say goodbye when the previous nanny left? Do the children still have a relationship with prior caregivers?

It is traumatic when a parent does not give children a chance to say goodbye to caregivers, and it means that the children have no closure when the relationship ends. There are only a few instances where even a simple goodbye hug is not in the best interest of the children. In most cases, being able to say goodbye is the healthiest choice. If children have not been able to say farewells to their previous caregivers, it might be difficult for them to bond with you because they will have a hard time trusting that you are not going to leave without warning.

Not every job is meant to last forever, but the relationship with the children can. The book *Like a Second Mother* by Barbara Blouin contains a history of over 40 caregivers written by the children they cared for. *Like a Second Mother* includes memoirs and photographs of each. This book and countless other stories of nannies continuing in the lives of their charges prove that when a job ends, the relationship changes but it can continue.

The Most Important Part

> "A work agreement is really a trust agreement." Glenda Propst

Every nanny position will have its ups and downs. It is genuinely impossible to address every topic so that there is no frustration. The best way to address any issues that arise is a work agreement. It is a *must* for any position, whether short- or long term.

Nanny Basics and Beyond

A work agreement is a document that answers the questions regarding all aspects of the job. It gives both you and the parent a place to reference when there are questions that come up, and there will always be questions that come up. It is a place where both of you declare your expectations of each other. It sets the job off on the right foot—everyone agreeing on the scope of the position.

There is no foolproof way to know exactly what a job will be like until you start it, and, even then, reality can change in the blink of an eye. Being a nanny can be fun, surprising, and rewarding, but it is also a lot of hard work. Not everyone understands what a nanny does, and it can be isolating. It is crucial to have support from your peers, whether from a local group or online, and associations for learning, support, and networking.

GLENDA PROPST

Glenda Propst is the owner of the blog and Facebook page Nanny Transitions. Her goal is to offer support, information, and resources for nannies who are going through the transition of leaving a family.

Glenda is a founding board member of the International Nanny Association (INA), the 1991 Nanny of the Year, and one of the three founders of the former National Association of Nannies (NAN). She is also a founding team member of the Regarding Nannies Development Team. In

Chapter 1. The Dream versus the Reality

2016 Glenda was awarded the Meritorious Service Award from the INA.

She retired in 2015 after 31 years as a professional nanny, but don't think she is going to disappear. Glenda has a passion for the nanny industry and will continue to work hard to educate and support nannies in every way she can. She is so excited about this segment of nanny coaching and is honored to be a part of it.

NannyTransitions.com

Nanny Basics and Beyond

Chapter 2. Work Agreements Matter

"Rather than thinking of a work agreement as a binding document that 'holds' a family or nanny to a set of rules, think of it as the tool that is the basis for building the nanny-family relationship." Michelle LaRowe

Michelle LaRowe of NannyTraining.com and Morningside Nannies discussed this very important topic with me. Michelle has been in the nanny industry for 24 years as a nanny, placement agency owner, educator, and leader. Michelle is a trusted champion of parents and nannies.

You need a work agreement for every position you accept. This sentiment will be repeated throughout this book. The work agreement encompasses every part of a nanny job and is the foundation of the working relationship you have with your employers. It does not matter if you have been a nanny for two weeks or 20 years, you need to have a clear understanding of your job duties and responsibilities.

In its basic form, a work agreement is a document that outlines all aspects of your working arrangement. It ensures that both you and the parent you work for have a mutual understanding of the terms and details of your employment. The work agreement can be used as a reference tool and protects everyone from misunderstandings. No one needs to rely on his or her memory of what was discussed or agreed upon because the details are all documented in writing. It often safeguards the relationship between you and the parent because having your agreement in writing minimizes miscommunication, which minimizes conflict.

Convincing Parents

When you bring up the topic of having a work agreement with your employer, you may find that he is reluctant to put your agreed-upon terms in writing. You can highlight the benefits of having a work agreement as well as your mutual interest of creating better communication. Help to educate your employer on the value this document holds—regardless of who is hired for the position.

Chapter 2. Work Agreements Matter

Start the conversation by explaining a written work agreement ensures that you understand and can meet the expectations your employer has for you. To do your very best work, you need to have a full understanding of what is expected of you.

> "This document can save a nanny-parent relationship. Nannies who have a comprehensive work agreement are more likely to stay long-term, so that means the parent avoids turnover."
> Michelle LaRowe

You can also highlight that having a work agreement is a proactive approach to your relationship, and can eliminate issues before they become problems. This approach attracts the best caregivers to nanny positions because professional nannies insist on having a work agreement in place before they start a job.

At times, parents don't know where to begin when it comes to drafting a work agreement. The good news is that, as a professional nanny, you can help by presenting a basic template that you develop together. If you work with a reputable nanny referral agency, it likely has work agreement samples that you can use. If you don't have a sample work agreement, you can find basic templates online or by joining the International Nanny Association.* Members of the International Nanny Association have access

Nanny Basics and Beyond

to a basic work agreement template as part of their membership benefits. However, you don't need a fancy document to draft a quality work agreement. A simple Word document that covers the topics below will work just fine.

Basics to Include
Define Agreement Parties:
- Your name and the parent's name (two parents if you are employed by both)

Dates:
- The job start date and expected end or renewal date

Hours:
- Times you are expected to be at the house and any additional "on call" hours (these should be paid)
- Minimum hours you will be working per week. (This is often referred to as "guaranteed hours," meaning that even if the parents do not use you for these hours, you are paid for these hours.)

Pay Rate:
- A base hourly wage rate. Nannies cannot be paid a salary
- An overtime hourly wage rate (see Chapter 3 for more details on overtime pay)
- An "on-call" rate
- An overnight wage rate (often a set price for sleeping hours, unless you are working

for a child who wakes often in the night, like a newborn)
- Travel rates (how compensation will work if you travel with the family)

Pay Period:
- When you are paid (weekly, bi-weekly, monthly)

Method of Payment:
- How you are paid (through a payroll service, direct deposit, or check. Cash is not recommended)

Late Charges:
- Consequences if you are late to work (are there a certain number of times you can be late before there are consequences?)
- Compensation if the parents are late coming home

Tax Responsibilities:
- The method that employers will use to withhold taxes needs to be clearly defined here.
- As household employees, nanny employers are legally responsible for paying half of your Social Security and Medicare. A number of states also require unemployment and workers' compensation insurance to be paid.
- Often nanny employers will agree to withhold income and FICA taxes as well. (There are several excellent companies that the employers can hire to do all the

work for you. Find more details in Chapter 3.)

Paid Time Off:

- These can be specific holidays, vacation days, and sick time.
- Be sure to state how the hours are accrued (annually, monthly, or by hours worked)
- When can they be used (e.g., are there days that you are not able to take off?)
- How are they to be scheduled (e.g., how much notice are you required to give for a vacation day?)
- It should be stated whether or not you are required to use days the family takes a vacation as your own paid time off or whether that is included in your guaranteed hours. I highly recommend that you require that *some* paid time off be at a time of your choosing, and it is incorporated into the agreement.
- It should also be noted how much notice the parent needs to give you if you are going to be off work without pay, and what happens if that notice is not provided.

Use of Sick Days:

- If these are separate from the standard paid time off, they should be listed here. If not, include a brief description of the expectations if you become sick.

Chapter 2. Work Agreements Matter

- If the parent would prefer that you not work when you are sick, this stipulation should be stated here. Parents who have children with special needs will often ask you to stay home if you are sick. Compensation for these days should be included here. Be sure to research your local laws, which may state that employees must have mandatory paid sick days.

Additional Benefits:

Other benefits include

- Access for you to do your laundry
- A cell phone or reimbursement for part of your cell phone plan
- Use of the family car during off hours
- Health insurance premium contributions
- Retirement account contributions
- Continuing education fund or extra time off for continuing education
- Commuting reimbursements
- It could also include access to a local gym or private club to which the family belongs. The parent can get creative with these benefits to entice you to accept a position as the nanny.

Expectations

Specific Job Expectations:

It is vital to clarify all details of the job. It can be helpful to create a bullet list. Be sure to include information about:

- Whose laundry are you responsible for?
- Are you responsible to clean and put away dishes?
- What other housekeeping jobs are you responsible for?
- Are you responsible for care of pets in the home?

Anything that will be expected on a daily, weekly, and monthly basis should be listed. If it is not listed, there should be no expectation of it being completed by you.

Children's Schedule:

This is a list of specific activities for which you are responsible. Activities may include

- Getting children to and from school
- Transportation to and from sports practices or games
- Tutoring
- Planning play dates
- Taking children to therapy appointments
- Taking children to doctor and dentist appointments

Children's activities can change from season to season. Be sure to keep an updated calendar so that all activities are easily tracked.

School and Activity Pick up procedure:

- School drop off and pick up process
- Names and phone numbers of teachers and other professionals in the children's lives

Chapter 2. Work Agreements Matter

- List procedures when picking up from additional activities

Emergency:

- What is the protocol when a child gets hurt and 911 must be called?
- Which parent should be called first and at what number?
- To which hospital should the children go?
- What are the procedures the parents want you to follow if it is a non-emergency injury?
- If there are food allergies or other special needs, having a detailed list of what to do in common situations is essential.

Emergency Documents:

- Emergency contact information for the parents
- Emergency contact information for family members
- Contact information for all doctors
- A completed Authorization to Treat a Minor Form
- A copy of the children's insurance cards

Basic Health:

- Are you responsible for keeping the child up-to-date with doctor and dentist visits?
- When the children become ill, can you make a doctor's appointment?

Food Restrictions:

- Include a list of food restrictions and allergies

Nanny Basics and Beyond

Special Circumstances
Live-in nanny:
- What are your living arrangements?
- Are you being provided with room and board?
- If you are being given room and board, that implies that you can eat the family's food when not working. If you are being given only room, then where should you keep and eat your food?
- Are there any expectations of you during off hours?
- If you use a family car, can you use it during off hours?
- Can you have visitors in the home and are there restrictions?
- What extra security should the parent provide for you?

Nanny who has his or her own children:
- Can you bring your children to work?
- Who pays for food and activities for your children?
- Where do your children sleep (nap)?
- Can your children play with the family toys?
- What other restrictions are placed on your children while in the family is home?
- You may want to consider making a note if the rules are different when the children do not come with you.

Separation or Divorce:

- If parents are separated or divorced, there are often rules and restrictions regarding your contact with a parent. Having a copy of the custody agreement can be helpful. See more in Chapter 18.

Travel:

- If you are expected to travel with the family, details and specific information for those trips should be covered here. See more in Chapter 23.

Household manager:

- If you also act as a household manager, this space should include additional restrictions or regulations around those duties. See more in Chapter 19.

Travel, Car Use, and Insurance

Travel with Children:

- Can you travel outside of the house with the children?
- What places can you go or are there any places that are restricted?
- What kind of advance communication do you need to give the parents when taking the children outside of the home?
- What mode of transportation should you use?
- Please note if the children in your care will be traveling in your car at any point, you will need to contact your car insurance company to determine if additional coverage is needed.

Clarify Vehicle Details:

- What vehicle will be used to transport the children?
- What insurance is used to protect you and children when you drive them around?
- How is gas or mileage reimbursed?
- Who will provide car seats and ensure they are correctly installed?
- Are there rules about food/drinks in the family's car?
- Are you responsible for keeping the car clean?
- It is also recommended that you have a tag or sticker on the child's car seat with the contact info of the parents in case of emergency.

House Rules

Off-Limit Areas:

Are there areas of the house or specific belongings that you and children should not use?

Restrictions While on Duty:

Are you allowed to

- Make personal phone calls
- Do personal errands
- Use personal electronics
- Access the internet while at work or even during naptime
- What are you able to do during naptime or while the children are at school?

Pictures and Social Media:

- Can you take photos of the children?
- Can you post pictures of the children, home, etc., on social media?
- Can you print photos for your use?

Food Management:

- Can you eat the family's food?
- Do the children have any dietary restrictions or allergies?
- Does the family have food expectations that you must also follow while on duty that might be different from your typical eating/food practices?
- Are you expected to eat with the children as a model for appropriate meal behavior and attitudes towards food?
- If you are to bring food to the home, are there restrictions, rules, or expectations involved?

All Aspects Relating to Operation of the Home:

You should have a basic understanding how to operate in the house. Things like

- The location of emergency shut-off valves
- Electrical breakers
- Flashlights/batteries and candles
- Fire extinguishers
- Medication
- First aid kits

You should also know how to

- Unarm and arm the security system
- Open the garage doors

- What to do if locked out of the house or car
- If there are pets in the home, you should know how to take care of them. Most nannies take on responsibility of caring for pets, but even if it is not always your responsibility you should know what kind of care they need.
- If someone spills something, is there a particular way to clean carpets, floors, or furniture?
- There could be a long list of things that you need to know about the house. Even if it pertains to areas of the house that are off-limits, you should have an idea of what to do in an emergency in that area of the house.

Disclosure of Video Cameras:

If the family uses video cameras to monitor the house and children during the day, the location of each camera should be disclosed here. A knowledge of the way these cameras and video will be used should also be included, e.g., is it a live feed or a recording? Be sure to research this on the local level as there are state and local laws that may apply.

Position Changes and Review

- The Frequency of Review:
- How often will you have a review and how often will wage increases be considered?

Chapter 2. Work Agreements Matter

The Process to Change Agreement Outside of a Review:
- Detail how either party goes about changing the work agreement outside of a scheduled review.

Notice and Termination Policy:

Topics for this include
- Process and requirements for the nanny resigning
- Process and requirements for the family terminating the nanny
- Notice required from either party should they wish to end the work relationship
- Specific actions that would constitute immediate termination

Nanny jobs in most states are considered "at will" positions. "At-will" employment is a term used in U.S. labor law for contractual relationships in which an employer can dismiss an employee for any reason without warning. The employer does not need to establish "just cause" for termination. It is better to have statements about immediate termination and any policies that would be instituted in your work agreement. In a situation like this, there might be an opportunity for the nanny to improve performance so that termination can be avoided. This section should explain how that would be managed and what expectations would need to be met.

Confidentiality Agreement

What can you disclose about where you work and for whom you work? A confidentiality agreement can protect both parties. It should outline the restrictions and should be revisited during the annual review, at which time it should be updated with any changes if required. The confidentiality agreement is often a separate document but should be summarized here as well.

Further Advice

Every job is different and will carry its own set of unique expectations and duties. The list above is a good stepping-off point for all long-term nannies. Temporary nannies may not need to include everything listed. As you and your employer have regular reviews, this document should be updated. If a change is agreed to in the review, it should be included in the new work agreement. It is a good idea for you to keep a running list of topics that you wish to discuss with the parent and possibly add to the work agreement.

Especially in the beginning of a new job you and parents should set up a weekly or monthly meeting to discuss how things are going. However, communication can happen through email, text messages, and phone calls. It is important to find what works best for both you and the parent.

Chapter 2. Work Agreements Matter

"Major conflict in a position comes from one or both parties being frustrated about something and remaining silent for too long." Michelle LaRowe

Communication is the key to a healthy relationship between you and your employer. Many nannies wait too long to bring up a problem because it is awkward; however, waiting only makes the issue more stressful when it is finally addressed. You need to say the words because your employer cannot read your mind.

Having a good work agreement can be a job-saver, but what if you are already in a position and you don't have one in place. Bringing it up on the anniversary of your start date can help. Stating that you want to sit down and have a review sets up the expectation that you are looking to improve the working relationship. It can also help to use "I" statements such as "I have been worried that I am not meeting your expectations and, to remedy that, I would like to put together a basic work agreement. That way we can both have a clear understanding of the position."

Verbal Agreements

Many nannies wonder if there is ever an appropriate time to have only a verbal agreement. There are times in the day-to-day operation of the house and caring for the children that you simply decide to do a seemingly minor task to help out the family. This is standard practice in a job where you are acting in partnership with the parents. However, you must be careful that a one-time circumstance does not turn into a regular expectation. If you sense that the parent is suddenly expecting something that is not in the work agreement, it is best to have a sit-down conversation with him ASAP to work out the expectation. If you are willing to add this to your work agreement, then it should be in writing. If not, then you should make that clear as well.

Breach of Agreement

One of the problems you will face is a family who does not hold up its end of an agreement. You should always discuss this sooner rather than later by asking for a meeting to discuss things.

Anytime you need to discuss a sensitive issue, start the conversation a positive statement. It can be about the children, the job, or simply how much you are enjoying a responsibility. Then you move to the issue at hand. Keep it short and straightforward using "I" statements as much as possible, e.g., "I have noticed that when I come in the morning, the dishes from the evening are not put in the dishwasher. I understand that you all have so much to do in the evening and getting those done is a challenge when all you want to do is spend time with your children. I am wondering if we can figure out a plan because while I don't mind helping out in this way every once in a while, having to put dirty dishes in the dishwasher adds stress and confusion to my morning with the children."

Sometimes you simply know it is time to move on or you know that the fit is just not right. In these situations, you should not have a problem giving appropriate notice (according to your work agreement) to your employer. This can be an uncomfortable situation, but, as caregivers of the children, part of our job, even when leaving, is to do so in the most professional and considerate way possible.

While most jobs can end with proper notification, not all of them can. A work agreement should be broken only if you feel endangered in some way and after you have thoughtfully considered the consequences. The repercussions of quitting on the spot and not giving proper notice do not end with the financial ramifications on this job. You may have to explain your choice for years to come.

Contract versus Work Agreement

There are two terms that are used to refer to the document we are discussing. These two terms are a source of great confusion. Many people use the term "work agreement," which is any written understanding between at least two individuals. Others call it a "contract." A contract is a specific type of work agreement that is enforceable by law. The reality is that while you could use a work agreement in legal discourse, it is not binding and would only be used to show each party's intentions.

Starting with a comprehensive work agreement will alleviate so many problems down the road. It should be specific to avoid miscommunication, and seen as a tool in the bigger picture of the working relationship. Relationships can only be healthy with a solid foundation, and that is achievable with a good work agreement.

MICHELLE LAROWE CONOVER

Michelle LaRowe has over 20 years of nanny industry experience as an award-winning nanny, former executive director of the International Nanny Association, nanny placement agency owner, and as the founder of NannyTraining.com.

Michelle currently serves as the editor-in-chief of Longhorn Leads, managing the content across its portfolio of nanny-related sites including www.eNannySource.com and www.GoNannies.com, in addition to serving as the executive director of Morningside Nannies, the company's award-winning placement agency. Michelle takes great pride in delivering high quality, CACHE-endorsed learning to nannies across the globe through her training platform, NannyTraining.com, and partnerships with organizations such as Nanny Stella, Inc.

and the international wealth management platform *rise*.

Michelle has contributed to TWINS Magazine, wrote a chapter for the best-selling *Experts' Guide to the Baby Years* and contributed a devotional featured in *Day Starters for Moms*. Michelle has also authored four books of her own: *Nanny to the Rescue!*, *Nanny to the Rescue Again!*, *Working Mom's 411* and *A Mom's Ultimate Book of Lists*.

Michelle is regularly called on by the media and popular parenting magazines and websites to share her expertise. She has been featured on Parents.com, Parenting.com, and BabyTalk.com, and has been a contributor to ModernMom.com, Momtastic.com, and other parenting websites.

NannyTraining.com

* Nanny.org

Nanny Basics and Beyond

Chapter 3. Getting Paid Legally

"I really encourage everybody to understand what your rights are under the law and be paid legally. There are so many advantages." Lora Brawley

I spoke with Lora Brawley of Nanny Care Hub about this often misunderstood topic. Lora has been working in the nanny industry for more than 25 years and is a devoted leader to the industry.

To many people, as a nanny, you are nothing more than a glorified babysitter. However, those of us in the nanny industry know the truth: You are a professional who invests in, cares for, teaches, molds, and helps to transform the next generation. You do more than watch the children in your care as they grow, you invest in their growth. This is a career that shapes the future, and yet you often continue to struggle to be seen as a professional.

Many employers of nannies still refuse to pay legally and even more struggle to understand *how* to pay caregivers legally. As a professional nanny, you are tasked with not only demanding legal wages but also educating your employer on the facts.

What It Looks Like

"Remember, get paid for every hour you work." Lora Brawley

So what does it mean to be paid legally? First, it means you are paid minimum wage or above. Minimum wage changes over time and varies from state to state, but at the time of this book edition the federal minimum wage was $7.25 an hour.

Being paid legally also means that you are paid for every hour you work. This includes overtime* pay, which for most household employees is any hours over 40 in a seven-day period. For these extra hours, you should be paid your normal wage plus an "overtime" rate, which is usually another half of your normal wage or time and a half. Be sure to do your research as laws vary in different locations and the laws surrounding domestic workers are changing.

Chapter 3. Getting Paid Legally

Parents might say that they want to "bank your hours" or "comp" your pay. "Banking" hours is when the employer pays for hours that you don't work and then you have to make up the hours later. "Comp-ing" your hours refers to the practice of not paying you the overtime you worked one week then giving you extra time off at a different time. It is not legal to be paid in either way. Truthfully, it works to erode the relationship between you and your employer because you might be expected to work 60 hours one week and only 20 the next. While it might be nice to have the stable income, planning your life around that schedule is demanding and ultimately disrespectful to your time.

HomeWork Solutions, a household payroll and nanny tax compliance service, shares this case study relating to legal pay and overtime.

Background:

A family hired a nanny full time to work 45 hours a week. They agreed to pay $720 a week, which they calculated as $16 an hour. Every week the parents paid their nanny and gave her a pay stub that showed 45 hours at $16 an hour. They did all the required tax filings on time and thought they were in great shape.

The challenge:

The family became dissatisfied with the nanny and fired her after ten months. The nanny filed for unemployment, which the parents felt was unfair since she didn't live up to their expectations. They thought she was fired for cause and fought the claim. Meanwhile, the nanny was equally unhappy, and when the family contested her unemployment claim, she consulted with her state's Wage and Hour board and filed a claim for unpaid overtime.

The situation:

The nanny argued that she should have received time and a half for her five hours of overtime hours every week, and she was owed the difference in back pay. The Fair Labor Standards Act (FLSA) states that "any employer" who violates minimum wage or unpaid overtime compensation laws may be liable for both the shortfall and liquidated damages. This means that the family could be responsible for double the damages. The amount was $40 per week, for 46 weeks, or $1840. This amount was doubled, and it was deemed that the family was required to pay $3680 in back wages. The family also incurred attorney's fees, since the parents paid for representation in the matter.

The solution:

This ended up being a very costly problem that could have been avoided if the parents had consulted with a household payroll specialist when they initially hired the nanny and set up payroll. They could have been coached on how they could have paid the nanny the flat $720 a week and state the wage in both hourly and overtime terms.

Chapter 3. Getting Paid Legally

You might also hear a parent say that she wants to pay you a "salary," which is paying you a more substantial wage every week but not paying attention to the number of hours you work. This is also not legal, as often you will be working for a significant amount of hours for which you are not being paid. While in many other professions being paid a salary is legal, as an in-home childcare professional, you are not exempt from FLSA (Fair Labor Standards Act), which means that you have to be paid at least minimum wage and overtime for every hour worked.

The last requirement for the nanny's fair pay involves taxes. Taxes are often a massive roadblock for many families. Many parents don't know where to begin and feel that paying the nanny's taxes is not that important. There is help for those that don't want to go it alone. Payroll services offer guidance in the form of articles and helpful tools for free. However, if the parents want to invest further and save time, they can hire the nanny payroll services to do a portion or even all of the work for them when it comes to nanny taxes and wages.

Educating Parents

There are compelling reasons for a family to want to pay you legally. First of all, if the employer is caught not paying her portion of the taxes for Social Security and Medicare, she can be facing civil and possibly criminal charges of tax fraud, not to mention that she will have to pay the taxes back to the IRS.

Another compelling reason for a parent to pay your tax is that it is an investment in you. For the best and most professional nannies, a job paid under the table is a non-starter. If a parent wants the best, she is going to be willing to invest in you to keep you around.

Perhaps the most influential reason for a parent to pay you legally is that there can actually be tax incentives to do so. While the parent is required by federal law to pay half the nanny's Social Security and Medicare taxes, she can often take advantage of childcare tax breaks and flex spending accounts through her employer's benefits, which can offset the cost of the Social Security and Medicare taxes. In many states, employers are required to pay unemployment and workers' compensation insurance as well.

What about the 1099 Tax Form?

A parent might say that she heard she can give you a "1099" form instead of a "W-2." A "1099" is tax form that is given to independent contractors at the end of the year so that taxes can be complete.

*The IRS says that "an individual is an independent contractor if the payer has the right to control or direct only the result of the work and not what will be done and how it will be done." Furthermore, the IRS states that

Chapter 3. Getting Paid Legally

household workers are rarely independent contractors. Independent contractors have control over the hours that they work, where the work is performed, what tools or equipment is used in work, and must be able to work for others during the same time. An example of an independent contractor is the landscaper that your employer might hire to mow the lawn. The landscaper decides when he will do the job, what tools are used to complete it, if other workers are hired, and he can do other jobs during the same timeframe.

The earnings of a person who is working as an independent contractor are subject to Self-Employment Tax. This means that independent contractors pay more taxes out of their income than employees because they are paying both the employer and employee taxes.

Care.com HomePay provides this case study on its website.

Mary has a gross wage of $630 per week. If she is paid as an employee, Mary is entitled to all benefits and protections under the law, including workers' compensation and unemployment. Her paycheck looks like this:

Gross Weekly Wage: $630
Social Security & Medicare ($48.20)
Federal Income Tax ($51.78)
State Income Tax ($28.64)
Total Tax Withholdings ($128.62)
Net Weekly Pay $501.38

Net Annual Pay $26,071.76

If Mary gets a 1099 and classifies herself as an independent contractor, she is not eligible for workers compensation if she is injured on the job or for unemployment should she be laid off. Her pay looks like this:

Gross Weekly Wage: $630
Social Security & Medicare ($96.40)
Federal Income Tax ($51.78)
State Income Tax ($28.64)
Total Tax Withholdings ($128.62)
Net Weekly Pay $453.18
Net Annual Pay $23,565.36

Not only did Mary lose her benefits of workers' compensation and unemployment but she is also losing about $2500 a year in taxes.

What Can Happen to the Family

If a parent pays you as an independent contractor, the IRS characterizes this as Employee Misclassification. If you are let go or injured on the job and file an unemployment or workers' comp claim and your employer has not been paying insurance, an investigation may be triggered. This could lead your employer having to spend thousands in back taxes. Your employer could even be charged with tax fraud. Plus if she has an unemployment claim against her, that will mean that her unemployment insurance will be higher in the future.

Chapter 3. Getting Paid Legally

"If you start a relationship with an employer and agree to be paid under the table, you are agreeing to break the law with someone that you don't even know." Lora Brawley

Paying taxes is not a choice. It is an obligation, and it is the law. Your employer might try to reason her way out of avoiding the nanny taxes, but don't fall for it. It is not worth the costs in the long run, for the nanny or the parents.

Many parents argue that paying nanny taxes is too complicated. It is true that it is an investment to set it up in the beginning, but the consequences for not doing it are too significant. There are also many companies dedicated to doing nanny payroll taxes. Most CPAs do not understand the nuances of the in-home employment industry, and have been known to give incorrect advice.

What Can Happen to the Nanny

For you, being paid as an independent contractor (with a 1099) means that you have to pay not only the employment taxes but also all of the Social Security and Medicare taxes that your employer should be paying. You will have added expense to your taxes because you are characterizing yourself as self-employed. Not to mention you will not have access to unemployment benefits if you are let go and workers' comp if you are injured. If you are hurt at work, there is nothing you can do if your employer will not help you pay for medical bills. If the family fires you, there will be no unemployment benefits because independent contractors are not eligible.

GTM Payroll Services provides this illustration relating to unemployment benefits.

Situation:

You hire a nanny, make sure to follow wage laws, and withhold Social Security and Medicare taxes. However, you didn't know that household employers also owe unemployment taxes. When your nanny is let go through an amicable split, she files for unemployment. However, the state has no record of unemployment taxes being paid.

Consequences:

The family can expect a notice from your state with failure-to-pay and failure-to-file penalties, which can add up to 50 percent of the tax due. That's on top of the unemployment taxes you didn't pay.

Being paid legally as an in-home childcare provider also means that you have employment verification. If you want to buy a car, house, or any other big purchase that you need to show proof of income, you don't have that if you are paid under the table. Even if you were paid with a 1099, lenders do not look highly on "self-employed" individuals and you may not get the loan you want. It can even prevent you from renting an apartment in some cases.

Being paid legally also means that you are contributing to your Social Security retirement account. The longer you pay into Social Security, the more you get out of it when you need it. If you go your whole career and never pay into it, you will not be able to utilize it in retirement.

Beyond the tangible benefits for nannies to be paid legally, there are the emotional reasons. It is the right thing to do, and it eliminates the worry that you may be audited in the future. Being paid legally can give you a strong sense of professional identity and make you feel that you are a part of the broader industry. So often nannies struggle to be recognized as professionals. Doing it the right way reinforces the fact that you have chosen a profession that is real and viable.

What You Can Do

> "Make a decision that you want to be treated like a professional, you want to invest in yourself, and that you no longer accept being a second-rate employee. You are going to stand up for what is right." Lora Brawley

If you are in a situation and you now know that you are not being paid legally, I encourage you to speak to your employer about it. It is going to be hard and your employers may be angry, but if this is your career and you want to be a professional, it is the only choice you can make.

Be ready that your employer may feel that you have misguided her and that you now want to change the agreement you had. For this reason you should be prepared to walk away from this unhealthy position. However, you also might be pleasantly surprised at the added respect you receive from your employer. If it means that you need to find a new job, you can do so with pride, knowing that you are taking yourself seriously as a professional. Don't let anyone tell you otherwise.

When you approach the parent, you need to go with the information on why and how this would be a benefit to her. You need to have clear reasoning and be willing to work out a plan with her. Even if that means that you compromise in other areas, it will be worth it. Sometimes it is your job to educate the parent in this area.

Payroll Companies

You may be asking what a payroll/tax company can do to help you. There are three companies I recommend: HomeWork Solutions, Care.com HomePay, and GTM Payroll Services. These companies can benefit your employer as little, or as much, the employer wants. They can be available to provide information. Their websites are chock-full of valuable tips, available

Chapter 3. Getting Paid Legally

without even picking up the phone. These companies can also offer tax service, developing and preparing what is needed to stay tax compliant. They can keep track of and calculate paid time off, and can even aid in wage payment, so that the employer does not need to remember to write a check every other week.

When working with a payroll company, your employer can choose as little or as much help as she wants. It is up to the employer, but education is powerful for the family.

Do the Right Thing

It can be tempting to accept a position where the pay is not quite right. The pressure you may face when dealing with bills and keeping yourself healthy is a heavy weight to bear. However, forgoing the "right" path is not only against the law but it means you are abandoning the protections you are afforded under that law. In the long run, doing the right thing is actually doing the smart thing.

LORA BRAWLEY

Lora Brawley of NannyCareHub.com is a 25-year nanny veteran, industry leader, trainer, and consultant. Lora specializes in helping nannies and parents effectively navigate the search and hiring process, creating fair and balanced nanny contracts, and building long-term, positive nanny-family relationships. She's earned a reputation for providing a unique blend of common-sense strategies and intuitive

53

guidance to the nannies and parents she works with. Lora is also a certified mediator, conflict coach, communications trainer, and positive discipline parent educator.

NannyCareHub.com

*1. Live-in nannies in many states don't get time and a half for overtime hours. https://www.homeworksolutions.com/knowledge-center/fair-labor-standards-act-flsa-overtime-rules-and-domestic-employment/)

*2. https://www.irs.gov/businesses/small-businesses-self-employed/independent-contractor-defined

Chapter 4. Writing an Effective Résumé

"You can have the most impressive skills, vast experiences, and a winning personality, but if your résumé, references, and portfolio have misspellings, wrong numbers, and other obvious mistakes, you will likely not get in the door." Erin Krex

I talked with Erin Krex, formerly of First Class Care in Chicago. In her years as a business owner, she has looked through thousands of résumés. She knows what stands out and what passes by.

Your résumé is often the first thing a prospective employer will see from you. It can impress with a professional look and well-thought-out words, but it can easily be mundane and ordinary. An effective résumé works to highlight your best qualities and experiences without oversharing details for which the reader does not care.

What Makes the Nanny Résumé Different

It is important to remember that this is not a business résumé. There are many templates you can find searching on the internet to help you create a business résumé, but many of these differ from what the nanny résumé should be. If you are applying as an office professional, the person hiring does not care what your likes and dislikes are. However, your résumé as a nanny needs to be more detailed regarding your background and passions. You need to explain throughout the document why you want to work with children. The big questions that the parent or placement agency will be asking when they read your résumé is why do you want to take care of children and are you going to be committed to it.

> "While fancy or obscure fonts might make your résumé stand out, it may not do so in the way you want." Erin Krex

Your résumé should be easy to read with professional text. Including fancy and obscure fonts or formats will only make the document harder to read.

Chapter 4. Writing an Effective Résumé

You may want to include a picture in your résumé, but you may decide not to. This is a decision you will need to make for yourself. If you want the parent to get to know the personality and accomplishments you have before the family sees your picture and starts making judgments, you should not include a picture. However, images can help make your portfolio memorable, and, if you choose to add a photo to your résumé, you need to make sure it is a high quality, professional headshot. Your résumé will not stand out with a low-quality photo of you that has been cut out of another photo. While your portfolio is a great place to add pictures of you with children, your résumé is not.

Crucial Components of a Résumé

You want your résumé to be a visual representation of how you intend to care for their children, with excellence and attention to detail. Each entry should be identical to the others in style and explanation. So the dates should be in the same place for each entry as well as the names and locations. Indentations should all be the same, as should the font type and size. These may seem like small details, but when a prospective employer is quickly looking at a résumé, you don't want yours to look sloppy. When a résumé does not have a clean format, it means that the human eye needs to work harder to follow the details. You don't want your potential employers or placement agency to have to work hard to read your résumé.

When possible, make edits to your résumé based on the information you know about the family to whom you are sending it. For instance, if you are applying for a job with older children, highlighting your previous experience with older children can be helpful. If you are sending the résumé to a family who travels, stating that you have experience traveling with children would be a huge plus.

Name and Contact Information

Your phone number and email address are necessary. Your mailing address is no longer required information, but the city and state you currently live in can be helpful. Note that if you work with an agency, often the agency will omit your email address and phone number when giving your résumé to a prospective employer to avoid having the employer contact you directly.

Phone number and email should be at the top of each page if there is more than one page. Make sure that your email address sounds professional and is not silly or inappropriate. If you need to, you can create an email address specifically for your work as a nanny.

Example:
Susie Winlock
susiewinlock@gmail.com
312-555-9876
Oak Lawn, IL

Chapter 4. Writing an Effective Résumé

Cover Letter

It should be short (less than 250 words.) This is to your chance to share the passion you have caring for children, what makes you a great nanny, as well as the professional and personal hobbies that will aid you in your job. If you love a certain sport or volunteer regularly, this is the perfect place to add that info, which can be edited for a specific position as needed. For instance, if you know that the family loves camping and you do, too, that would be an important thing to add. List your unique cooking skills or second language abilities if you have them. If you are applying as a nanny/household manager, computer skills can be necessary. If you have an older child, listing your volunteer experience with after-school tutoring will be a huge plus. When you talk about your hobbies, stick to the hobbies that you have had in the last five years, because the family wants to know what you are doing now.

Example:

I am excited to be applying for the position with your family. The following details will list my qualifications for the position, but because I will be caring for your children, I know that you want to know a little more about who I am.

I have been working as a professional nanny for six years, and I often say that shaping future leaders is the best and most important job in the world. It is a responsibility I take very seriously.

In that time, I have cared for children from six months through age ten. I have worked with children overnight and taken several vacations with the family.

I am committed to continuing my education in the field of childcare. I have become an INA Credentialed Nanny and keep my CPR and First Aid Certification current, because I believe that safety in the home is critical. I am always looking for ways that I can expand my knowledge and stay up to date with changes to the science of child development.

I understand the struggle that parents face as they look for a nanny to care for their precious children. My goal in the home is to partner with you. Leaving your child with another adult is not easy, but I hope to ease that emotional struggle and help your household run more smoothly.

Thank you for considering my application.

Education and Achievements

In this section of the résumé, you will provide a well-organized list of completed education or achievements. You will explain any job-related continuing training that you have or any industry exams or credentials you have passed. For example, if you passed the INA Credential Exam or attended conferences or seminars related to the industry in the past, add these experiences to the list. Be sure to say if you have a current First Aid or CPR certification too. If you have space, you can list the most influential workshops you have taken or workshop that might stand out to that particular family. Be sure to provide a website for each school or activity you participated in so that potential employers can look up those achievements. A potential employer will love to see your continuing education because it demonstrates that you invest in yourself.

Under each experience, you should give a one sentence explanation of what it is. Remember, this list can be tailored to each family, according to its makeup and its priorities.

Example:

2008-Current—www.nannypalooza.com www.nanny.org

Attended 15 Nanny Conferences over the last ten years. INA Conference, Nannypalooza and National Nanny Training Day. In total participated in more than 75 continuing education workshops focused on a variety of topics related to caring for children, such as Smart Sleep Solutions for four months and up; Infant Brain Development; and Sibling Rivalry: More Friendship, Less Fighting.

Job History

In this section, you will provide a well-organized list of previous professional childcare experiences. You should name your earlier jobs in the childcare field. Start this list with the most recent job you have had.

You will not need to list every job outside of the industry, but you should explain any gaps in your childcare experience. You will want to include the starting and ending date of each position, as well as the city, state, or country the job took place, and the children's ages. Then you will give a 3- to 4-sentence explanation of the specific features of the job. You should also include the reason for leaving the position.

Your job history is a great place to make adjustments based on what you know about the family you are interviewing as a potential employer. For instance, if you are interviewing for a family with three active young children, adding more detail to a similar job description can make a difference. If you are interviewing for a family who has a child with exceptional needs, making sure to point out that you have cared for a child with similar needs before can help. Be careful not to reveal confidential details. While you should explain what you did in the job, specific locations and names should not be disclosed. While a former employer might not mind you using her last name on your résumé, a potential employer or placement agency might see it as a break with confidentiality.

Example:

December 2005-August 2010, Skokie, IL

I provided full-time, in-home care for one child who was three years old when I started.

This boy had exceptional needs, and I was charged with administering breathing treatments, medications, and keeping thorough records of everything. I did in-home teaching in his early years, since he was too ill to attend school. I was able to teach him through fun and exciting games in a hands-on learning environment, as well as numerous adventures outside of the home. This position ended when the boy was able to go to school.

February 1997-October 2005, Chicago, IL

I provided full-time, in-home care for three children who were five, three, and one. I provided meals, creative activities, engaging play, and exciting excursions for the children. In addition, I did the grocery shopping, laundry for the children, scheduled and transported them to extracurricular activities, and did many long-term overnights with them. As the boys got older, my role became one of a household manager, and I added more household tasks to my job description. This position ended because the family moved out of state.

References

A potential employer and placement agency will want to talk to at least a few individuals who you have worked for in the past. The references you give are just as important as your résumé and the interview. You need to select people who not only have first-hand experience working with you around children but have wonderful things to say about you.

The best references are past employers with whom you have left on excellent terms. However, if you are just starting out in the industry, you might not have too many parents you can call on to be your reference. In that case, a person you worked with in a volunteer capacity around children will work. You should avoid using a personal family member or close friend as a professional reference.

Before you list anyone as a reference, make sure that you check with that person to confirm that it is OK to give out that name and contact information. It is important that when a potential employer contacts your reference, the reference is aware that the call will be coming. If you have had people listed as references for a long time but have not been actively looking for a job, be sure to reach back out before giving their names out again.

The list of references should be separate from your résumé. There will be people who you want to give your résumé to that you don't necessarily want to have the list of names and phone numbers of your references. You can say on the résumé that references are available by request.

Nanny Portfolio

A Nanny Portfolio is a bound document that you bring with you to in-person interviews. It is your chance to showcase your areas of expertise in more detail.

Contents of the Nanny Portfolio should include your résumé, references, and several letters of recommendation; some of these letters can be from your references. You should have copies of certificates from any conferences, seminars, or other training programs that you have completed. Your CPR and First Aid Certification should be in there but only if you are current in your accreditation. If these certifications have expired, it is better to note when you plan to become recertified.

In addition, contents of the Nanny Portfolio can include things like weekly sample menus, an example of your detailed activity journal, and sample lesson plans for the week. Your portfolio is the place to put the photos of you working with children. Be sure to get parents' approval (in writing) before placing photos of their children in your portfolio. Don't make the entire book about pictures, and remember that potential employers like to see you working with children more than they want to look at "selfie"-style pictures.

Your Nanny Portfolio does not have to be expensive or fancy, but it should have a professional look. I recommend that you have the portfolio printed and bound at an office store, but you could also use an inexpensive three-ring binder and still achieve a professional look.

If you show up to the interview with a Nanny Portfolio, you show that you are proud of what you are doing and the potential employer will usually remember you. You should show the Nanny Portfolio to the parent and walk through the different sections together.

You may feel awkward when you watch the parents read through your Nanny Portfolio in the interview. There are a few ways you can relieve this pressure. If it feels appropriate in the moment, you could ask to use the restroom, which will allow them to look through the document while you are out.

Creating a unique mini portfolio for each interview can give you the chance to personalize it for the family you are meeting, and will alleviate the awkwardness of the parents feeling that they need to read through the entire thing while you are in front of them. If you know that part of the job would entail preparing meals for the family, you could include a weekly sample menu that you put together for a previous family. If you know that the family is looking for a nanny who will focus on education with the children, you could include weekly lesson plans that you put together. This mini Nanny Portfolio would have copies of a lot of what is in your full portfolio, minus any personal details that you would not want to leave at someone's house.

If you go with the option of a mini portfolio, you need to be aware that you will likely not get it back. While some people have had luck with leaving a self-addressed and stamped envelope for the family to return it to you with, it puts pressure on the family to remember, which might not send a great message.

Top 5 Résumé Mistakes

"You can have the most impressive skills, vast experiences, and a winning personality but if your résumé, references, and portfolio have misspellings, wrong numbers, and other glaring mistakes, you will likely not get in the door." Erin Krex

Proofreading

I cannot stress to you enough the importance of proofreading your résumé. There are tools to help you online and you should use them, but nothing beats finding a friend or colleague who is a self-described grammar fanatic. If you don't have a family member or a friend who can help, hire a qualified editor or even barter with someone for his or her time. It is an investment you need to make for your résumé.

Gaps

If you have blank spaces (more than six months) in your work history, you need to provide an explanation for those in your résumé. Potential employers and placement agencies will notice, and they will wonder what happened. Be honest and positive. Never take a job off your résumé because you are ashamed of the experience. If there is a simple explanation, then you should add that to the history because people will assume the worst. They are always going to think that you're hiding something.

Negative reasons for leaving

Sometimes a job does not end well. Sometimes you need to leave the job, and sometimes the family asks you to go. You should always be honest on your résumé, but if you paint the reason you left as a negative, that will turn off a potential employer. Avoid using phrases like "I needed more money" or "the family was mean." This will only highlight your negativity.

Instead, find a constructive way to say that you left a job that was negative: "I left the position because I had outgrown the job." "The job was no longer a good fit for me." "I was ready for a change." If you were asked to leave a job, you could say, "I was let go because I was no longer a good fit for the family," or "The family decided that they no longer needed me."

Too long

Rarely should a résumé be more than two pages in length. If you have a large number of positions to list, you might want to consider listing just the dates, names, and locations of all but the last few, most recent entries. Then you can explain those in more detail. Parents do not want to sift through more than two pages on a person. Ideally, the résumé should be a front-to-back single page if it is printed.

Social media checks

The social media check has less to do with the résumé itself and more to do with what the parent and placement agency will do as soon as they have read your résumé: They will get on their computers and put your name and information into a search engine. What they find will determine if they move forward with an interview or if they put your résumé to the side. It is so crucial that you keep all public social media tasteful and you are not seen doing anything inappropriate. The reality is that a potential employer cannot control what you do outside of your work hours, but he is considering entrusting you with his children. If he goes to your Facebook page and see pictures of you from spring break living it up, he is going to think twice about moving on to the next interview with you. You want to make sure that the only pictures that anyone can see are suitable for family viewing. If you have publically embarrassed former nanny employers, a potential employer is not going to want you working for him. Stay positive on social media as if everyone in the world will see it someday because chances are...they will.

In closing, a well-written, professional résumé is essential to get you to the next level.

The chances of getting there are slim if you don't have a great one. Erin shared with me her thoughts on the process.

> "It's like dating—résumé, photos, they are paper—it's only when you meet someone that you get a true sense compatibility or fit." Erin Krex

ERIN KREX

Erin owned First Class Care nanny placement agency for nine years, where she not only placed nannies but also worked with parents, giving them guidance and advice on childcare decisions. Erin is a Certified Baby Planner and received her training at The International Maternity Institute. She is a member of the International Academy of Baby Planner Professionals as well as the International Baby Planner Association. In her time with First Class Care, Erin was an active member of APNA (Association of Premier Nanny Agencies) and was on the INA (International Nanny Association) Board of Directors for four years. She has been a recipient of the Leading Moms in Business award for three years and also holds the title of 2010 APNA Agency of the Year winner. As an agency owner and working mother with domestic help, Erin frequently writes and speaks on subjects related to employee best practices for both families and employees. With her 12-year-old son, Erin founded Brick Loot, a monthly subscription box company.

www.BrickLoot.com

Nanny Basics and Beyond

Chapter 5. Navigating the Interview Process

"Interviewing with the family is just as much about making sure that you want to take the job as it is for them to make sure they want you to take care of their children." Donna Shannon

I spoke with Donna Shannon of Personal Touch Career Services about the interview process. Donna is an accomplished career coach and one of the few people who understands the unique struggles within the private service industry.

The word "interview" often brings up strong emotions for people. Most people find interviewing a nerve-wracking and have a fear of the process, but it does not have to be. If done with confidence and understanding, it can be more of a form of art than something to lament.

Types of Nanny Interviews

When nannies are looking for a job, there are a few kinds of interviews they will go on. The first might be an interview with a nanny placement agency. This is generally an agency that has a physical presence within the market it serves. That community can be a particular town, city, or state. It could also be a particular niche in the worldwide marketplace. Quality placement agencies should want to meet you to interview personally. Agencies that are worldwide might instead require a series of face-to-face interviews over the internet.

The second type of interview is with a potential employer once you have been matched through an agency. At this interview, the placement agency will have given the family pertinent details about you and the placement agency should have also given you details about the family, but it is likely that you have not personally spoken before this meeting.

The third type of interview is one that you have with a family who you found outside of a placement agency. Perhaps it was an online recruitment service, or you answered an ad. Maybe the family received your contact information through word of mouth. You don't know that family well, and for safety's sake, you should have spoken on the phone at least once before you go to an in-person meeting.

Safety Tips

When working with a placement agency, there are specific safety tips you should keep in mind. There are several advantages to working with an agency that has a presence in your community. Most are established and, because they live and work in the community, are usually safer to get a job though than by other means. However, you should do your research on the agency and make sure that it is reputable. Check how long it has been in business, and if it is involved in professional associations like the INA (International Nanny Association) and the APNA (Association of Professional Nanny Agencies)*. You should be meeting with agency employees in an office building or public location, never in a private home.

When working with an online recruitment site or via word of mouth, there are other things to keep in mind. It will be necessary for you to do more work vetting the family. You may even need to coach the family through the process.

For safety's sake in this situation, it is essential to have two separate points of contact before you meet with parents in their home. First, talk with the family over the phone and then meet with the parents in a public location, like a coffee shop (one that is quiet) or a library meeting space. A parent's business office would be OK as well. The children should not be present for this first, public meeting.

The third interview can be in the family's home with the children present. However, even after speaking or meeting with a potential in two separate points of contact, you should give a family member or trusted friend the address where you will be and ask that person to check in with you after the interview is scheduled to be over. If at any point during the interview you feel uncomfortable, politely excuse yourself and leave. Trust your gut. No job is worth being put in a situation where you are unsafe.

Messages before an Interview

In this fast-paced, shorthand world, we often forget that the first impression people have of us is via email and text. It is possible to make a good impression via an email or text message. Proofreading a message to potential employers or agency staff is vital. Look the message over and make sure that not only are there no misspelled words but that the point you are trying to make is clear. If this is something that does not come easily to you, you might want to have a friend or partner who is willing to review your writing. There are even online resources that are free and can help get all the spelling, grammar, and punctuation right. Even the shortest message that you send provides an impression of you. Make it a good and professional one.

Conversations on the Phone

The phone interview is an important part of the process. A bad phone interview can mean that the family does not pursue an in-person interview. It can be hard to get a good sense about a person from phone call, but here are things that will help impress a potential employer.

Make sure you are talking in a place that has reliable cell coverage (if you are using a cell phone) and that it is quiet, with few distractions. If you are in a pinch, sitting in a car with the windows closed can usually be acceptable. You should not be driving a vehicle or stopped in a noisy area.

Be sure to ask lots of questions about the children in this first conversation. A potential employer wants to know that you are interested in the children's likes, dislikes, and temperaments. Talking about what the family enjoys doing together can really help you find mutual topics of interest. You don't need to go too in depth with questions at this point.

Answering questions thoroughly but efficiently on the phone is probably your most important goal. Being on the other end of a phone instead of the other end of the couch means that you can take a breath before you answer the question, and do so with clarity and composure.

Though the phone interview is usually used to ascertain if schedules will match up and personalities will mesh, wages might also be brought up by the parent. It is important to note that the parent might be turned off if you bring up money this early in the process. If you did not work with a placement agency, you may feel it is a necessary topic so that you don't waste anyone's time. It is best at this time to just ask a general question looking for a range to be sure you are on the same page. If the potential employer gives you a range that is outside what you are willing to accept, don't continue beyond this first interview. Everyone's time is too valuable to lead the parent on, and, in this digital age, that can quickly become problematic.

Preparation before the Interview

Prepare before the conversation begins. A potential employer can tell when you just show up without any preparation. Keeping a well-organized list of the families you are interviewing with is a helpful step. Whether you use paper and pen or prefer to use a digital organizer, have a system and know what it is. Be able to pull up details about the job in just a few seconds. And bring these documents with you to the interview. You should also bring your Nanny Portfolio and either a mini portfolio (as discussed in Chapter 4) to leave with the family or an extra copy of just your résumé, letters of recommendation, and references that the parents can keep. Print everything on high-quality paper using a good printer.

Do your research on the family. If you are using a placement agency, ask as many questions about the family as possible. The family will likely research you on the internet. You should do that too.

Be rested. It is a horrible feeling to walk into an interview tired. Avoid this at all costs. Try to plan your day so that you have a little bit of downtime right before the meeting. No one looks good when she has been rushing around trying to get the interview.

"Knowing how you are going to answer the first question gets rid of a lot of nerves." Donna Shannon

Practice your introduction. Most families ask the same types of questions at the beginning of the interview: Tell me about yourself? Why are you a nanny? Why do you want to take care of my kids?

Practicing how you will answer these questions is helpful.

You should also practice the hard questions you know you will be asked. If you have a gap in your employment history and you know that will come up, practice how you will answer questions about it, over and over again. If there is a question that you have been asked in interviews before that made you stumble, practice what you will say. Practicing your responses will help you build your confidence.

> "An athlete will make sure that her muscles are warmed up before a match or game. Repeating tongue twisters helps warm up your tongue to speak, but the benefit goes even further. Correctly saying tongue twisters requires you to concentrate on the words you are saying. In essence, practicing wakes up your brain and gets it to work in conjunction with your mouth, which helps you answer questions quickly and efficiently."
> Donna Shannon

Five minutes before you walk into the interview, practice saying difficult tongue twisters. They can be simple phrases or more complex sentences.

- Toy boat (repeat)
- How much wood would a woodchuck chuck if a woodchuck could chuck wood? (repeat)
- Red leather, yellow leather (repeat)
- Ed had edited it (repeat)

Take a deep, slow breath just before you walk in the door. Your body's natural reaction, when faced with a stressful situation, is to take shallow, quick breaths. This is the fight-or-flight part of the brain. Unfortunately, these shallow, rapid breaths tend to cause the heart to race and then more stress is put on the body. By consciously stopping and taking several deep, slow breaths, you send a message to your brain to calm down. Making an effort to do this just before you walk into an interview can force your heart rate to lower and make you appear calmer than you might feel.

Attire for Interviews

For your meeting with a potential employer or placement agency, your clothing should reflect the position for which you are interviewing. What you wear should be comfortable, but you should not be too casual. The clothes you wear should also make you feel powerful and in control.

Dress within your personality, choosing neutral tones or solid colors when possible. Mixing strong colors or different prints can draw the eye to what you are wearing rather than your qualifications. Black and white, while not considered neutral, are power colors.

Dress conservatively in business casual. Do not choose anything too tight or revealing. Clothing that is meant for a night out with friends is not clothing that should be worn at an interview.

What you wear sends a message to potential employers. Make sure that your clothing is clean, pressed, and tidy. If you look like you just rolled out of bed, that makes you look like you are too relaxed, even sloppy or messy. You need to find a balance between appropriate and your personality. What you wear once you have the job may be more relaxed depending on the family's expectations. For the first meeting with the children, you can dress more comfortably, but your clothes should still be conservative and appropriate.

Wear closed toed shoes, not sandals. Make sure you wear socks, tights, or pantyhose. Parents often want you to remove your shoes at the door (it is a good idea to ask them when you enter). It's not appropriate to be barefoot during the interview, even if family members may be barefoot themselves. Make sure there are no holes in your socks or stockings.

Avoid wearing large amounts of perfume. In fact, if you can, don't wear any perfume at all, since many people are highly sensitive to smells and this can turn the potential employer and the children off right away. Do not chew gum or suck on anything during the interview. Many people find this rude and it will be a distraction from you.

Be Prompt

Being on time is essential. Your timeliness is the first impression you are giving with the family or placement agency. A no-show sends a genuinely horrible message to prospective employers and will likely mean that you will not be placed with an agency. You should not be too early or too late. Being early means that you might be inconveniencing the family, because they are not ready for you. Being late makes them wonder how often you would be late for work. It is a good idea to leave extra time to get to the location of the meeting, but then drive around and wait to arrive in front of the house until a few minutes before the appropriate time. This way you avoid being late because of traffic or an accident, but you also don't show up before they are expecting you.

If you are running late because of traffic or another unavoidable situation, call the family as soon as you know you will not be on time. Giving this warning will mean that the potential employer is not waiting at the door. Most people will understand the situation and be appreciative of your call. If you work with an agency, you will also want to call your contact there so he or she knows the reason you were late, should the parent mention it.

Canceling the interview for anything less than a true emergency sends the wrong message. It says to the potential employer that your schedule matters more than her needs. If an emergency does occur and you absolutely must cancel, contact the family as soon as possible. Be honest about the reason you are canceling and what the crisis is. Apologize for the inconvenience and then give the parent several alternative days and times that you could make reschedule. If working with a placement agency, be sure to inform its staff of the change.

Your Answers

Speak clearly and slowly. Make eye contact with both parents if they are interviewing you. Sit up with legs straight (or crossed at the ankle). You don't want to slouch in the chair or take your shoes off unless that was asked of you at the door.

Don't be afraid to take a minute to pause and think about your answers before speaking. People get nervous when asked a question that they don't know how to answer and end up stammering for a few minutes. This usually causes the interviewer to lose interest in the answer and sends the wrong message.

It is important to state your opinion clearly and with conviction. Knowing why and how you care for children should get you excited. However, it is equally important to know when to stay silent. It can be easy to over-share and babble, especially when you're nervous. This can turn off parents almost as much as not answering questions at all. You should always stay on point and not veer off the subject.

While stories of your childcare experiences can add value and show your expertise, you want to be careful not to share confidential or sensitive details about previous families. Parents will listen, and then wonder what you would say about them if you took care of their children.

If the topic turns to pay, continue to state your expectations within a range of wages and benefits. A potential employer will often want to have you narrow your wage during an in-person interview, but unless you are genuinely willing to start the negotiation in this tense situation, it is best to finish the discussion and collect your thoughts before you consider a more specific package. You can use phrases like "I might consider that in the right circumstance," and "with the right benefits, I would consider it" can help move the conversation along.

Be careful not to undercut yourself here or state a range that you know is outside of the family's range. If you go too high, you might discourage the employer from hearing any more from you, but if you state a price that is really low, she will lock that into her brain as the price she can pay you.

Your Questions

"Interviewing is a reciprocal process. You want to make sure that you would be comfortable working with the family. This is just as important as making the parents feel confident in trusting you with their children." Donna Shannon

Most interviews start with questions from the parents or placement agency, but you should have questions ready to ask the parents as well. When the parent answers the questions you ask, watch her body language. It can tell you more about the answers she gives than the words she speaks.

Ask the family if you can speak to the previous nanny or past babysitters so you can talk with that person about the children. Asking this question can be empowering, and the family's willingness to allow this can be a significant indicator of the job.

Meeting the Children

As a primary caregiver for the children, you should meet the children before you accept and start any position. There are very few exceptions to this, but they include newborn, travel, and temporary jobs. In fact, having at least one meeting with the entire family is more than just a good idea. This process gives you the opportunity to see how the family interacts with each other. It can also reveal how the household works and give you the chance to observe how the parents communicate with each other and with the children.

If it is at all possible, you should require seeing the house before accepting a position. It is valuable as well to observe the environment in which you will be working. How tidy is it usually? Is it free from clutter? Are you comfortable working in that type of environment? Where do the children play or work? Where is the laundry done, folded, and put away? Will you be walking up several flights of stairs to put away clothes and toys several times a day?

Thank You Note

The message you send after the interview can be almost as valuable as everything mentioned above. Sending an email or text within 24 hours after an in-person interview will not only tell the family members that you are courteous and kind but will keep you fresh in their minds as they continue to meet with additional nannies or as they are making their decision. It can also be a chance to follow up with any questions they asked or to ask additional questions that you forgot in the interview.

The process of interviewing can seem overwhelming, but it does not need to keep you up at night. By preparing, practicing, and pumping up, you will be ready to totally impress potential employers with your professional attitude and style.

DONNA SHANNON

Donna Shannon, President of The Personal Touch Career Services, is one of the few career coaches in the United States who understands the unique nature of the private service industry. Drawing from both her corporate recruitment and luxury market placement experience, she has been helping job seekers with professional writing services, job search consultations, and classes since 2004. Her book *How to Get a Job without Going Crazy* (2nd Edition, 2012) is available on Amazon.com. Donna is based in Denver, Colorado, and works with job seekers across the country and abroad.

PersonalTouchCareerServices.com

* TheAPNA.org

Chapter 6. Choose the Right Job

"Nannies usually believe they have a good grasp of their strengths and weakness, but often these preferences can get cloudy with the pressure of the job hunt." Marcia Hall

A great nanny-family match depends on just a few factors: What the family is really looking for and what type of nanny you really are. Notice they both have to do with reality. Reality versus perception is what we will look at as we discuss how you choose the job that is right for you.

A parent might think he knows what he wants in a caregiver for his children. These assumptions often end up pretty far off the mark. He may say he wants a nanny who will focus on the care of his children, but, at the end of the day, he also values a clean and well-organized home. You may believe you have a good grasp of your strengths and weakness, but often these preferences can get cloudy with the pressure of the job hunt.

Unique Relationship

To choose the right job, you need to have a good understanding of the unique relationship you have with the parent who employs you. This relationship will always be work. It will mean sacrifice and compromise from both parties. All relationships involve these to a degree. However, the nanny-parent relationship requires a level of understanding that is unique.

A parent who employs a nanny might have feelings of guilt about leaving and perhaps even jealousy at the relationship you are building with the children. These feelings can often sneak up on the parent and catch everyone off guard. To make the relationship work, those emotions need to be acknowledged and processed.

As a nanny you walk a line that can be hard to see. You need to provide excellent care for your charges, be loving and caring, but you need to be careful to not step over that line and offend or hurt the feelings of your employer in the way you care for the children. This line is so difficult to see because it often changes. Most days the parent can be happy that you were focused and loving, while other days feelings of guilt and frustration rise with these same acts of love. This tense situation is one of the biggest reasons this relationship is so unique and may change from day to day or family to family.

In this chapter, I will discuss several factors that should go into the decision about which job you should accept. As we go, it is important to visualize what it might be like to work for the family described. Be honest with yourself. Is this a situation you could handle or is it one you would find too challenging? Make a note of each dynamic, style, or condition you know you could *not* manage. Also, make a note of each for which you may be slightly uncomfortable.

There is nothing wrong with deciding you would not want to take a position for one of these reasons. It is part of knowing yourself and who you are as a nanny. Moreover, remember that, as in any relationship, you cannot change a person. You can only change how you respond to that person. In this circumstance, you can choose if that is a person who you want to work for or not.

Basics Before You Move Forward

There are a few fundamental subjects that you need to think about before you start questioning the parents. These conversations could reveal deal-breakers for you and would mean that you would not be able to accept the position. Nannies should be up front about their expectations on these topics, so you don't waste your time or the family's time. However, many of these questions can be off-putting to a potential employer if you bring them up too soon. Particularly questions involving wages and benefits. The parent wants to know you care more about the children than the money.

Here are a few simple questions to ask during the process.

- What is the wage range that you are willing to pay?
- What is your understanding of legal pay for nannies, and are you willing to adhere to that?
- Are you willing to pay through a nanny payroll service?
- What other benefits would you consider?
- What is the basic schedule or hours that you would like the nanny to keep?
- What are the primary tasks in the home that you would like the nanny to complete?
- How long do you intend to employ a nanny?
- How would you like the nanny to handle emergencies?
- How do you like to communicate on a day-to-day basis with the nanny?

History of Care

The family's child care history is more important than you might think. It can mean the difference between a great first year that leads to many more or a few awkward and frustrating months with a family. Understanding what type of caregiver this parent has utilized in the past can be a helpful indicator of what type of family you are looking at and what the parent is looking for in a nanny. Remember that the generalizations below are not always the case, and that you need to see beyond the answers for a clearer view of the family.

If this is the parent's first child, she is likely to be a "by the book" parent. She will be the type of parent who reads every parenting book, magazine article, and have an opinion on every child-rearing philosophy. She may question every doctor to figure out what she is supposed to be doing with her child. This is a broad assumption, and it is possible to find laid-back first-time parents, but even a parent with the most relaxed temperament will, from time to time, feel overwhelmed. I have never met a first-time parent who did not have at least a few moments of uncertainty.

If the family has had children in daycare previously, this parent is used to his child being on a very rigid schedule. He may or may not like this structured schedule. Regardless, you need to remember that the children are used to this stricter routine and if you deviate very far from a structure that they have grown accustomed to it will cause the children's behavior to change and usually not for the better. So, if you don't like structure and keeping to a schedule, this job might not be great for you because, at least at first, you will need to keep to the plan.

If the family has had only good experiences with nannies, the bar has been set high, and you will want to be ready to meet or exceed it. You will be judged by the level of care and organization established by the previous nanny. This job requires a nanny who does not quickly get jealous or offended. Parents may say things like, "Our last nanny did it this way. Why don't you?"

If the family has had only horrible experiences with nannies, you are not off the hook. It may seem a family with awful examples of nannies would be very easy to please. You may find this to be the case, but you also may find yourself compared to the other nanny. Parents might be reminded of the past nanny's negatives and be overly critical of your similar behaviors.

If the family has had a string of nannies, this could be a red flag that this employer is hard to please. It is best to get to the bottom of the reason for frequent changes in childcare. It could also mean that the parents have had horrible luck and bad judgment. In this case, children may not easily attach to you, and you will spend significant time building trust with the children.

If a parent was staying home and has recently returned to work, that parent will likely have significant adjusting to do. You will want to be extra patient and understanding about the guilt that she might feel.

Another kind of parent is one who relies on the advice of friends on every topic—from car seats to how to treat his nanny. This kind of parent might discount what you say and instead follow only the advice of his friends.

There are other types of family situations. These are just examples. When interviewing you need to trust your instincts about a situation that seems off.

Here are a few examples of questions you can ask in an interview that can help you better understand the family's history of care.

- Tell me about your previous child care experiences.
- What were the things you liked best about your previous nanny or daycare?
- What were your least favorite things about your previous nanny or daycare?
- May I talk with your previous childcare providers?
- What are negative stories you have heard or fears you have about having a nanny?
- Where do you go when you need advice about parenting?

Parent's Work Schedule and Location

Where, how often, and how long the parent works can help you discover the nature of the job. You may have a stay-at-home parent who needs extra help. This family is looking for an employee who will provide an extra set of hands during the day. This position is oftentimes called a mother's (or father's) helper, and is an excellent job for a nanny starting out who has limited experience with children. However, it may not be right for you if you value your independence or have been an independent nanny for a while.

You may have a work-from-home parent who is home but in an office most of the day. This situation can work when the parent gives herself firm boundaries or when the home office is far away from the children's play areas. It can be challenging for young children, especially if the house is small. Both the parent who is trying to work and the child who is trying to play can easily distract each other. It is often difficult for a parent to ignore her upset child and not intervene, even if she trusts the caregiver. Discussing these boundaries and having a solution before accepting a job is necessary. Solutions to this problem are numerous. You and the at-home parent could communicate via text when the child is upset so you can reassure the parent that all is well. Frequent outings can also resolve this problem. This situation is not right for every nanny. It often takes a forthright person with good communication skills to ensure boundaries remain set.

You may have one or two parents who both work outside the home with rigid schedules that don't often change. This can mean that a parent

Chapter 6. Choose the Right Job

is almost always home on time. However, if you need flexibility in your schedule, it might not be a good fit because the parent will struggle to find someone to cover the time you need off.

You may have one or two parents who both work outside the home but have very flexible schedules that often change. Working for a family with flexible schedules can be nice. You will be more likely to have days off suddenly. Be sure you include these details and their outcomes in your work agreement. Securing your days and time off is usually much more manageable. However, this parent is more likely to change schedules at the last minute and come home late with little or no warning.

You may have one or two parents who both work outside the home for very long hours. You should be very well paid for this type of job because of the long and stressful hours. If you take a position like this, be sure to discuss overtime compensation with the family. This type of job will be challenging. It is vital for you to cultivate a life outside of work. Having a job with long hours will make it difficult for you to develop a life outside of work. If the parent is willing, you could solve this problem by hiring a part-time babysitter. This way you are not so overworked, and you have backup care if needed. You can offer to search for and help hire this person.

Regardless of the kind of family you choose, it frequently falls on you to find solutions to problems that arise. This list is not exhaustive, and you will often find variations of these examples. There are more types of jobs and more dynamics that you will need to decide if you are OK working with. Parents' work schedules and habits will significantly contribute to the relationship you have, and these work schedules should be discussed at length with any potential family.

Here are examples of questions you can ask in an interview that can help you understand the parents' work schedule and location.

- What is your typical work schedule?
- How often does your work schedule change?
- If you work from home, do you want to set a specific time in the middle of the day to interact with your children?
- If you work from home, how would you like me to communicate with you?
- If you are home when I am here, how would you like me to handle issues with your children if they question my authority or are asking for you?
- If you work long hours, would you consider hiring a babysitter to help me with the hours?
- How often do your hours change and would you want me to stay if you were suddenly home from work?

- How much notice do you need when I need time off?

Parental Partnership Style

Partnership style refers to who is in charge of the finances and day-to-day running of the house. Some partnerships find one parent in charge of the majority or all of the family decisions. It can be a challenge if the parent who makes the decisions is not the parent with which you have the most contact. Cultivating a good working relationship with both parents is crucial. It can also be valuable to address concerns with both parents. It means you need to be comfortable talking with both.

There are partnerships where both parents share in the decision process. This situation can be great, but be aware that parents who fully share decisions of the family need to be able and willing to connect and agree with each other most of the time. Otherwise, you run the risk of becoming the middleman to their inability to communicate effectively.

If one parent makes financial decisions and the other makes day-to-day, running-of-the-house decisions, you will find that you are required to discuss different topics with a different parent. You will also need to make sure you have a good rapport with both parents. If you are uncomfortable or overly nervous interacting with either parent, this might cause problems.

If you find that one parent makes all the decisions and the other is left to follow those decisions, tread carefully. While this dynamic can be used to hurt and abuse, it can also be a positive experience for both individuals. This is often a cultural or religious choice that is made by both parties. While it may not be the choice you would make for yourself, be careful to not judge others for their choices. However, if you feel that you are unable to work in an environment like this, the job is not a match for you.

Understanding partnership dynamics in a marriage or relationship can be very challenging. If you had a happy and uplifting childhood, you would likely be most comfortable with the family dynamic in which you were raised. However, if your past includes painful memories of how your parents interacted, finding a job where you work with parents who have the same dynamic might trigger feelings of fear and anger.

Don't underestimate how vital this information is when you work with parents. As the nanny, you will be their partner too. If you don't understand how they work together, it will be tough to find your place in the relationship. In some situations, one parent can play the nanny against the other parent. Do not let this happen. You have to make it very clear that you will not take sides in any situation.

Here are examples of questions you can ask in an interview that can help you better understand the parents' relationship with each other.

- If I have issues with day-to-day problems that arise with the children, to whom should I talk?
- If I have issues with the business aspects of the job, to whom should I turn?
- What type of role would you like the nanny to have in the family?

Home Living Arrangements

Whom the children live with will undoubtedly make a difference in the relationship you have with them. It should also be carefully weighed into your decision to accept a position or not. Some families have two birth or adoptive parents who live together. It can be a very positive experience if the parents work to keep their relationship healthy.

Other families include two parents who are co-parenting from separate homes. This includes parents who are separated or divorced but not remarried. Many times in this situation, the parents share equal time with the children. They jointly make decisions—both financial and day to day—regarding the children. Most likely, in this case, you would technically be employed by both parents, and so would need to discuss issues with both. It is important not to exclude one parent from the decision-making process. It can be a great job, but beware that you do not become the middleman in the relationship.

Nanny Basics and Beyond

At times families have a single parent who has custodial care of the children, but the other parent has regular visitation with the children. This is a couple separated or divorced, and the parent with custody has not remarried, and you are likely employed only by that parent. Firm boundaries need to be set by you, so that you are not put in the middle of what can be a tense relationship. Take care even in situations where the parents seem to get along well, especially if the separation is recent, because things can change quickly.

If you interview with a family where the children live full time with one parent but have sporadic visitation with the other parent, you will want to understand the nature of your relationship with the other parent. The other parent may, or may not, have open and frequent communication with the children, but for a variety of reasons, the parent is not seen often. Maybe the other parent lives far away or is just not a good influence on the children. The other parent could even be in the military and away for long stretches at a time. Single parents without strong parental support can often be overwhelmed. This single parent may be looking to the nanny as an outlet for friendship. If the parent needs that and you are not comfortable with it, it may not be the right place for you. However, a nanny can provide a valuable and welcome support for a single-parent home.

Chapter 6. Choose the Right Job

There are families with a single parent where the child never or almost never gets to visit or communicate with the other parent. There may be an underlying issue with the other parent that is not discussed. It is necessary to know how the parent would like you to handle questions about the other parent. Does she want you to discuss it with the children if asked? Does she want to have you refer those questions to her? This is an excellent place to encourage an honest conversation with the children. If there is a lot of secrecy surrounding the topic of their other parent, it could be a source of stress for the children, and having a conversation with their other parent can help a lot. It may be emotional for a nanny to work with this type of family, especially if your own personal history might trigger negativity. However, these children could use a nanny who has been through the same type of situation, as long as you are emotionally healthy and aware of the possible triggers.

Still other families are composed of a single parent, where the other parent is deceased or has no connection with the family. Issues here will depend on how long ago the other parent passed away or was disconnected. The manner of the disconnection will also factor into it. If the disruption was recent, the job will take an extraordinarily compassionate nanny to help the family deal with the loss. This job should be taken very seriously and only accepted if you are in a mentally healthy place from which you can help the children heal.

Then there are blended families that often mix a lot of the characteristics stated above. Children in blended families live with a parent and step-parents. The legal parents might have joint custody, or the children might live with one primarily. Blended families bring many benefits as well as challenges to you as the nanny. Benefits for the children can include having numerous adults who are excited about being involved in their lives. However, adding stepparents to a family can bring out strong emotions from everyone involved, especially the children. Blended families for the nanny can mean another boss to please and even additional children at times. The connection all of the parents will be a key to making the situation manageable. Understanding how each parent sees you in the lives of the larger family will also be critical. Having a system of communication where information can be efficiently transferred within the group is important. This job will not last if you don't have a good method to communicate day-to-day needs but also concerns that come up along the way.

There are endless ways that families are blended these days. The point is that the children's living arrangements dramatically impact the job and how you work within the family. If you were raised in one of these situations and had a positive experience with it,

Chapter 6. Choose the Right Job

you might be the perfect person to step in and support this family. Taking a job because you feel bad for children who are in a situation you lived though could be helpful, but you need to gather all the information you can about the situation. There may be surprises of which you were not aware. A position that you don't fit in will eventually cause you to burn out.

Here are examples of questions you can ask in an interview that can help you understand the living arrangements of the family.

- Tell me a little bit about your family and extended family.
- Tell me about the relationship your children have with their other parent.
- What type of contact would you expect the nanny to have with the other parent?

Personality of Parents

Personality can be a huge indicator of whether or not you will work well in a family or not. I encourage everyone to take a professional and recognized personality test. Not just those you find on social media. It will help you get to know yourself better, and it will also help you understand with whom you would work best. By exploring and understanding the different personality types, you can begin to pick up on the personalities of others.

I recommend people take one of the many tests from Consulting Resources Group*. The Consulting Resources Group has a personality test that is reasonably short and to the point. The company also has several other tests that I have found beneficial to myself and to my clients.

Another that I recommend is one that is now known as the Clifton Strengths for Students*. This test is quite a bit longer, but it will give you a more in-depth understanding of the specific talents you have and how you can use them in your career.

Taking these tests can help you clarify your skills and the tasks that you excel in. They are also very valuable to you as you look for a job because they can help you determine the personality styles that you will struggle to blend with and those with which you will outright disagree. Remember, though, that working for a person with a different temperament is not in and of itself a bad thing. If you work with someone who thinks, reacts, and works differently, that can be a good thing. It can mean that you will be able to provide a well-balanced experience to the children. However, respect for each other is vital to making the situation work when you are vastly different from your employers.

Here are examples of questions you can ask in an interview that will help you better understand the personality of the parents.

- What is the most crucial part of child development to you?

- What are your goals for your child?
- What are your personal and family values?
- Do you want me to immediately contact you if the children have a bad day or if particularly good happens to them?
- With what personality do you work best?

Ages and Personality of the Children

One nanny might love snuggling and playing with infants while another would go stir crazy if not out and running around. If you have a particular preference for age, number, or gender of the children you care for, it is important to remember that when looking for a job. You don't want to accept a position where you will eventually not be happy. It is not fair to you, the children, or their parents.

It is imperative, though, to take time to evaluate those desires, and it might even be a good idea to reconsider what you think your preferences are. You may be surprised to find that you would enjoy working with ages or personalities you have not considered or experienced in the past.

Here are a few examples of questions you can ask in an interview.

- Tell me a little bit about your children and what they like to do.
- How do your siblings get along together?
- How does your child get along with other children?
- How does your child get along with you?

- How does your child get along with other adults?
- What does a typical day look like in your home?

Parents' Expectations for Activities

The rules parents have for their children will significantly affect you. If parents have expectations with which you are uncomfortable or disagree, you should know before you accept a position.

Knowing the parents' rules for these topics will help you envision what your day-to-day life will be like with this job. Parents might have specific rules in the home that could be a deal breaker for you, or it might be your preferred way of working.

Here are examples of questions you can ask in an interview.

- What are your five non-negotiable family rules?
- What are the screen usage rules?
- Are there any dietary plans that need to be followed due to food allergies or preferences?
- Do you have any restrictions or expectations that I should know about regarding toys, language, or homework?
- Does the family use organic food, and non-toxic products and toys?
- Is there a second or preferred language spoken in the home?

Chapter 6. Choose the Right Job

- Are there any restrictions on playing outside of the home?
- Is there a focus on extra activities, like sports, the arts, or dance?
- What is your discipline philosophy? Why have you chosen this technique?
- How would you handle it if your child was found drawing on the wall? How you would like the nanny to handle a similar situation?
- How would you handle it if your child began arguing with another child on the playground? Moreover, is this how you would like me to manage the same type of situation?
- What do you do when a child "talks back" to you or other adults?
- If there is a discipline issue that I do not wholeheartedly agree with you on, how would you like me to handle that?
- How open are you to your child interacting with other children?
- What types of activities do your children do out of school?
- What are the top 5 rules you have for your children and family?
- Are there firearms in the house? If so, what safety precautions have been set up to prevent accidents with your guns?

Nanny Basics and Beyond

Exceptional Children
Working with a family who has a child with exceptional needs can be a challenge in many ways. It can also be one of the most rewarding jobs you will ever have. Knowing you are helping a child who is struggling can give you a sense of worth. No words can adequately describe what it is like see a child overcome obstacles others barely notice. The sense of accomplishment you receive knowing you're helping the parents is fantastic. However, this situation is not right for every nanny, and there should be *no* shame in that. See more on this in Chapter 19.

Here are examples of questions you can ask in an interview with a family with a child with exceptional needs.

- Tell me what worries you most about your child?
- What are your child's most significant struggles in day-to-day life?
- How can your nanny best support you with these needs?

Lifestyle, Religion, or Political Beliefs
These are tricky topics for a nanny to approach. If the parents you are interviewing with have strong beliefs that contradict your views, you have to ask yourself how comfortable you are with the situation. Can you spend a significant amount of time with a family who you strongly disagree with politically? Do you think you can help raise a child to believe in a god in

which you do not believe? Would you be comfortable working for a same-sex couple?

Part of the role of the nanny is to support and encourage the beliefs the parents have for their children. It is not your place as their childcare provider to disagree with the parents. It is your job to provide a united front. If you are unable to teach the children the religion their parents believe, you should not be caring for them. If you roll your eyes every time a parent discusses politics, the child *will* notice, and it will cause problems. If you strongly disagree with any part of the lifestyle of the parents for whom you work, it is not the right family for you. A professional nanny position is not the place to convince someone else that your own opinion is right.

Being honest with yourself and the family is important. Our beliefs tend to seep into everything we do, and when these beliefs are strong, it is almost unavoidable that the family will experience them. Working with a family who has completely opposing religious or political opinions can wreak havoc on the relationship. If you strongly disagree with parents on any significant issue, you should not work as their nanny, even if you think you can get beyond the problem.

Here are examples of questions you can ask in an interview to determine if the family has strong beliefs that you disagree with.

- As a nanny, I would never want to undermine what you are teaching your children about faith, politics, or life. Are there any beliefs to which you hold firmly that you hope to instill in your children?
- What are these beliefs and what would you expect your nanny to do if your children asked about these topics?
- Do you have any specific dress code to which you expect the nanny to adhere?

Know Yourself

Choosing the right job is the key to a successful career as a nanny. I have known many nannies who walked away from the profession simply because they kept taking positions that were not right for them. Start your job search knowing who you are and what you want. Interview with the intention of finding out what the family really needs from its nanny. Don't be afraid to pass on a job where you suspect you will be unhappy. At the same time, don't be scared to say "yes" to a job outside your comfort zone. You may learn something.

* CRGLeader.com
* StrengthsQuest.com

Chapter 7. Before Your First Day

"Give the same amount of respect that you are looking for from them and, if you are in the right place, that respect will come back to you." Marcia Hall

The first day of a new job is exciting and exhausting all at once. You have ridiculous expectations that your employer will always be on time, your charges will always be on their best behavior, and you will always be excited to wake up to go to work. However, it usually is not long before the honeymoon of those first few days and weeks wears off and the little frustrating circumstances start showing up.

This chapter will focus on what you need to know to set yourself up for a successful first day and beyond. In the last chapter, I shared with you that it all starts with excellent communication even before you get the job. That communication is even more important as you prepare to begin your first day. I cannot stress this enough: do not start a position without a written work agreement that outlines not just the basics but so much more.

There are several typical topics of frustration that nannies tend to face in any job. We are going to go through each one and discuss how you can work with the new family to address these issues before they become a problem. Remember that great communication starts with listening and putting yourself in the other person's shoes.

Running Late

As the nanny, you hope the parent you work for will always return home at his scheduled time. However, that is often not possible. Just as your job and traffic dictate what time you arrive home, so does his. Situations arise in the office that mean he cannot leave on time. Traffic might not cooperate on the way home. Remembering this perspective goes a long way in helping resolve this issue.

Start by explaining to the new employer that you understand there will be days that he is just not able to make it home on time. Let him know you will do your best to be flexible. However, you would appreciate as much warning as possible when this occurs. Come up with a system in which you communicate with your employer when you have a day that your schedule requires you to leave precisely on time. Perhaps this system includes a reminder text message in the afternoon so your boss remembers that today's the day when you need to leave right at 5 PM. In return, you can ask that if he suspects that he will be running late, he will notify you as soon as he can. This may not work 100 percent of the time, but when you express your understanding that work life does not always cooperate with plans, he will be more understanding of your needs.

On-Time Pay

This can quickly become one of the most divisive issues that nannies face and can make an amazing work situation feel like the worst job out there. Of all the topics you discuss on a daily basis with your work family, receiving your pay on a timely basis is also often the one that nannies dread talking about the most.

You hate to get to the end of the week, expecting to get paid, only to have the parent walk in and forget it is payday. All you want to do is get out of there and go home. Your heart races while you quickly decide if you are going to ask about it or leave and email him instead to avoid the confrontation. No one wants to go through that.

The best solution for this is to persuade your employer to work with a payroll service.

There are countless benefits to using one, from tax prep to consistent pay. Payroll companies take the worry out of the situation for everyone. If you can add that into the work agreement, it is well worth the effort, because it truly benefits everyone.

The three most popular companies in the industry today are HomeWork Solutions, GTM Payroll, and HomePay by Care.com. All three of these companies specialize in nanny-family work arrangements and are experts in understanding domestic employer requirements and employee rights. I encourage you to call each company with a list of questions. That way, you can go to your next interview armed with the information you need. Employers might say that they have a CPA that they work with, but the reality is that many CPAs work for large companies and don't understand the unique laws governing the nanny industry.

Your employer may not want to go that route. He may choose to take care of taxes and wages on his own. At the very least you need to have in writing when you are to be paid: at the end of each week, bi-weekly, or monthly? You need to know what to expect.

You can ask to be paid at the beginning of the day, rather than the end. We all know that the very end of the work week is crazy. You can ask your employers if it would be helpful for you to send a reminder email or text them the night before your payday. This can really help because it is so easy to get distracted by children in the evening.

You do not need to use a payroll service to take advantage of auto pay. Most banks now offer online bill-pay so your employer could set this up to automatically send your wages. It could be done by issuing a check on set days or transferring money from his account to yours. Ask your employer if he would be open to this system.

Bottom line: get this figured out before you start. Communicating your desire to make things simple for them will help.

Petty Cash and Reimbursements

In almost every nanny job there will be unexpected activities or projects that require the nanny to pay for something out of pocket and then be reimbursed. This area of friction can be resolved with several simple tools.

The first tool is a credit card linked to your employer. If the parents are uncomfortable with you having a credit card with no limit, they can purchase a pre-filled card. They can even set it up to put a certain amount of money in it each week, month, or when it is empty. Credit cards can be a easy way to make sure that you are not out extra cash for an extended period. It does have its drawbacks though. Many places do not take credit cards, which would mean you have to get cash advances. You will also need to be vigilant in keeping track of credit card receipts,

117

as it is easier to misplace them when you do not need to be reimbursed. One more drawback to this solution is that if the family has a low credit rating, it can have a negative impact on your credit rating.

Another solution is a petty cash envelope that is always kept with "X" amount in it and has a ledger to keep track of what is spent, when, and for what reason. This too has its drawbacks. Keeping cash in the envelope can be a challenge for the parent. For nannies, it might slip your mind to make sure the remaining money gets back in the envelope at the end of the day. If you choose this route, it is wise to keep the petty cash envelope in the same place every day and to give the parents a warning when it needs to be replenished. Be sure to keep a copy of each receipt for your own records.

Another method is to get a credit card yourself that you use only for work-related purchases. This can solve the problem of you needing to pull from your own resources to front the money for work expenses. It is easier to keep track of how much you spent because you simply show the parents the bill at the end of the month, and you are more likely to be careful with receipts because otherwise you are not repaid. You would then ask them to give you a check for the balance before the payment is due. If you go this route, it is best that you never use this credit card for any personal purchases because it will be confusing.

Chapter 7. Before Your First Day

If you are reimbursed for out-of-pocket expenses from the parents, it is recommended that you *not* combine the total with your weekly wages. Weekly wages and out-of-pocket expenses should be kept separate because while wages are taxable income, these reimbursements are not. You should recommend that the parent make a note of which is which on each check for tax purposes.

Regardless of the method, make sure to discuss any monthly limits the parents wish you to keep and then be respectful of that limit.

Job or Schedule Changes

Your employers may have started out thinking they only want you to clean up the children's toys, dishes, and clothes. However, they may quickly realize that there were additional responsibilities they would like you to do. Starting the job off with an open line of communication in regards to changes in schedules or services can help.

If you are willing or able to change your schedule, let them know. You need to make clear what your limit is. How flexible can you be? Be honest, because it does not help either you or the parents if you are not. If there are household responsibilities that you are not willing to ever do, be up front about these.

Often, the parent's expectations of what he requires change over time. It is rarely his intention to hire you and then switch the job requirements. It is almost always an issue of not understanding what he truly needs.

Work-from-Home Parents

In our digital world, more and more parents can work from home at least part of the time, so this situation is becoming more common. Parents who are at home during working hours can pose several complications. If you work for a parent who is regularly at home for any part of the workday, you need to set up boundaries before you take the position. Discuss with the parent how he wants you to communicate throughout the day, if and when he would like to have time with the children, and what you should be doing during those visits.

A parent who works from home or stays at home may want to be able to spend time with his children during the day. Sometimes nailing down a specific time is a challenge for him. You can encourage the parent to recognize that it will be a more natural transition for the children if this time is set each day. If that is not possible, it is vital to the emotional health of the children that they are given notice when daddy is going to "appear" and play with them for a bit. Children do not do well with surprises, and, unless they are told specifics about what is happening, it will be confusing. These surprise visits will also make the parent's return to work an even more traumatic event.

Chapter 7. Before Your First Day

It is important to point out that highly sensitive children might not do well with visits like these. It can be helpful for the first week or so to ask that these visits are put on hold until you and the children have found a good rhythm. There are children for whom the midday visit from mom or dad will never work well. The children will spend the 15 minutes being very clingy and acting out. Then, when mom or dad prepares to leave, there will be a massive meltdown, destroying the rest of the day. The best thing to do is to ask that you and the parents watch for signs that this visit might be too much for their children and discuss what the signs of trouble might be.

Another issue that tends to arise from a parent at home is when the children hear the parent or see him in passing. Children might be happily playing when all of a sudden they hear their father talking on the phone, or see him walk past the playroom. It is an inevitable and oftentimes unavoidable situation. After all, the parent who works from home does not want to be trapped in his room all day. But what if a child starts to cry really loudly? Talk with the parent about how he wants you to handle the situation *before it happens*. Reassure the parent that you will have the situation under control. Ask that he call or text you before stepping in to resolve the situation. Offer to send a "this is why she is crying" text when a child cries.

Nanny Basics and Beyond

A parent of young children who nap will need to be aware of nap time. If the parent's office is close to the children's room, the parent will need to try to keep noise to a minimum when the children are sleeping.

Family Rules and Discipline

Understanding your employer's perspective on discipline is vital to every nanny job. You should not accept a position where you disagree with a parent's strong philosophy about discipline. However, it is often the case that the parent's opinions change as time goes by or even that yours do.

It is also commonly the case that parents want you to disciple the children in one way and, whether intentionally or not, end up not following through on those rules themselves. Perhaps the best way to resolve this issue is to find out the parents' "top five most important rules" regarding discipline.

Ask them to give you the five family rules that are not negotiable. If the parents are unable to come up with five non-negotiable rules, you can offer to work with them to come up with the rules together. Below is a list of potential family rules. This is difficult, but boiling rules down to the top five and being on the same page with the parent when it comes to discipline is important.

- Consider others' feelings first
- Solve problems with your words
- Find a kind way to say what you need to

122

Chapter 7. Before Your First Day

- Work to heal relationships that have been hurt
- Work hard and do your best
- Be honest and tell the truth
- Show forgiveness and grace
- Treat your property with care
- Treat other people's property with respect
- Work together
- Be grateful for what you have and don't focus on stuff you want
- Specific limit to TV or other electronics
- Ask permission to borrow other people's belongings
- Knock on closed doors before entering
- Always use please, thank you, you're welcome, excuse me, etc.
- Use good manners at the dinner table
- When inside, use your inside voice
- Walk inside the house
- Don't talk back to adults
- Keep yourself clean
- Keep your room clean
- Clean up after yourself

By asking parents to pick through the multitude of possible house rules, you will help them narrow down their priorities and understand their perspective. Parents and nannies will always have certain behaviors that trigger a response more or less than another. It is OK for you to feel stricter about a rule being followed than the children's parents do, just as the reverse is OK. To set yourself up for success with the family, you need to have clear and established family rules.

That does not mean that the children will not be asked to do other things when their parent is home or when you are there. However, those five rules are important and universal. If you don't agree with *all* of those five, you are not in the right place.

Being Respected

Many nannies feel that they don't get the respect that they deserve from their employers. While you can't control what someone else thinks of you all the time, you can make decisions that will help parents see you a favorable light.

- Be a model employee. Always arrive to work on time.
- Show love, compassion, and protection to your charges and give them your undivided attention when you are there.
- Do things around the house and with the children that make the parents' lives easier and provide the parents with a chance to spend time with their children.
- Support the parents' decisions about discipline and child-rearing.
- Be sensitive about parents' emotions regarding guilt, jealousy, and control.

- Be a partner with your employers in raising the children and don't assume you always know what is best.
- Don't undermine the parents' authority.
- Educate yourself on the specific needs of the family. For example, if you are taking care of a child with ADHD, become an expert on the subject.

The biggest key to gaining respect from your employers is to always be willing to compromise. Give the same amount of respect that you are looking for from them, and, if you are in the right place, that respect will come back to you.

Rules for the Nanny

The families you work for may pay you to do a job, but they also invite you into their home. Imagine leaving your home every day and having someone else come to live there while you are gone. This would be a challenge for just about everyone, yet, this is what the parents you work for do.

Parents can be particularly strict about what they will and will not allow you to do while you are in their home, where you can go with the children, where you can wear your shoes, what you can eat, and many other issues. While this can be frustrating for you because you spend so much of your time in that place, you also need to be respectful of their space.

Starting a job off right means that you fully understand where your employers' boundaries are for the home. Can you talk on the phone or text while caring for the children, or can you only do so when the children nap? Can you use the computer, exercise equipment, or shower? Are you allowed to nap when the children are napping? Can you have guests over? Do the parents need to meet your guests? What foods are you not allowed to eat? Can you do personal errands with the children in tow? Don't just talk about these rules, get them in writing.

General Communication

No matter what happens, there will be issues that come up as you begin to work with a new family. Many useful tools will make daily contact easier. It is important to decide on an agreed-upon means of communication. Whatever you choose, make sure the parents will use it; otherwise, it is pretty pointless.

It can be easy at first to ignore those small frustrations, especially when starting a new job. You want everything to go smoothly, and you are putting your best foot forward. However, those small frustrations often become larger problems. Once it is a big problem, it is harder to resolve.

If you have a simple and open line of communication with the parent you work for, it is much easier to address any problems you have quickly. Whenever you approach your employer with a problem, there are a few things you should be sure to do.

Always be respectful. Communicate that you understand your employer's perspective and that he is not doing anything intentionally. Pose the concern as your problem, not his. State that you want to find a solution with which everyone can be happy. Use "I" statements, like "I am struggling with the long hours." Always be willing to alter what you do to find a solution and always say, "How can I help fix this?" Don't present a problem without offering a potential solution. Solutions are often left up to you anyway.

Work Agreement

The lack of a work agreement should be a non-starter for every professional nanny. It is vital to have a good understanding of every aspect of the job, from the care of the children to the pay and benefits received. Do not start a position without a work agreement in place.

Be Prepared for the Children

Having well-behaved children all the time is not a reality. However, there are effective tools that you can use to make the first few days and weeks go well. These tools will help you create a lasting connection with your charges.

Starting the job off right means that you quickly connect with the children. If the parent allows it, arrive the first day with an extra bag of toys, crafts, and books. The library and a dollar store are great resources for this and will not cost you a lot of money. Choose books and activities that you anticipate your new charges will love and that you enjoy too. Plan on doing this for the first few weeks and then allow it to taper off. You don't need to be bringing your tools forever. As you get to know the children, you will likely work together to have these toys, books, and games in their house.

With the parent's approval, plan a big outing where you take the children to a fun place within the first few weeks. This place might even turn into your "special" place, and that will work to establish a secure connection between you and the children.

Your Rules

Help the children in those first days to understand your values and unique expectations of them. You should always adhere to those top five rules that you worked out with the parent, but having a conversation about the things that are important to you can help them feel more secure in your care because they know what to expect.

Show extra compassion to the children during this transition. I am not suggesting that you allow them to get away with things on that top five list or that you don't follow through with consequences; however, there needs to be an adjustment period. You don't want to be too harsh in your first few weeks.

Chapter 7. Before Your First Day

The children are going to have legitimate questions about this "new person" taking care of them. Validate their concerns and start to get to know who they are. As you work to understand them, you are sure to fall in love with who they are.

It can be hard to find the balance between stern and sympathetic in the first few weeks, but I believe that while you are adjusting it is better to err on the side of compassion. It is relatively easy to amend discipline guidelines, but it is tough to connect with children when their first experience with you is severe.

Allow for time to play and to get to know each child. Though you want to have a fun first few days with your new charges, it is also important to find time to play with each child on his or her own. It is especially necessary to have one-to-one time with older children so that you can get to know them better.

Sometimes older children are less excited about a new caregiver, and it can be a challenge to find a way to connect with them right away. If the family has multiple children, you might suggest that you spend a few hours alone with each child during the first few weeks so that you can focus on getting to know that child on an individual level. I have found this to be a helpful introduction, and it makes each child feel special.

Adjustment

Expect to have an adjustment period. Don't be surprised if you find that after a few days, the excitement of someone new and exciting wears off and your charges start becoming more challenging. This happens especially with older children, who tend to be more resistant to having a "caregiver." Until you have been able to establish your dedication to them, older children can keep you at arm's length, especially if the children have recently lost a caregiver they loved or if they've had caregivers in the past who don't stay long.

Be understanding and empathetic. Don't push yourself on the children who do not want you and avoid seeming resentful if they push you away. Allow the children to feel angry that you are there and give them time to come around. Be consistent in your actions, even if one child is acting out toward you. The more consistent you are, the more the child will begin to trust in your stable presence.

Think About You

You can be so focused on a new job that you lose focus of yourself and forget to enjoy your time outside of work. You can become so attached to a family, particularly the children, that you feel like they are your family. It is OK to feel attachment; after all, this is the very nature of your job. I believe that without attachment, you are not thoroughly doing your job. However, it is crucial to continue to develop your life outside of work.

It is a delicate path the nanny must walk. You must connect and invest in the lives of your charges without threatening to replace their parents. This is a challenge that can only be accomplished if you have a healthy life outside of work.

New jobs can be difficult, and there can be days when it seems like the situation will not get any better. If you are struggling and feel that everything is a mess, look for the positive aspects of the job. They are almost always there, hiding in the places you least suspect.

Nanny Basics and Beyond

Chapter 8. Your Review

"The ever-changing journey of your nanny profession contains milestones and checkpoints. Many are fond memories of wonderful times, and others are memorable challenges. The annual and regularly scheduled performance reviews, along with your work agreement, can be tools that help you if you approach the process with confidence and knowledge."
Becky Kavanagh

I talked with Becky Kavanagh, from Heartfelt Parent Coaching, about this topic. In her 28 years as a nanny and parent coach, Becky has helped both parents and nannies through the review process.

Nanny Basics and Beyond

Longevity with a family has a great deal to do with the course you set when you first accept the job. Sitting down and working out the details of the work agreement is your starting point, providing the boundaries for the journey with the family. Along the way you'll hit milestone markers, one being the review.

If possible, including an annual review and other performance reviews into your work agreement will get everyone started on the right path. Then, as you approach those milestones, you are already prepared for the discussion with your employers.

The uniqueness of the nanny-family working relationship makes the review process equally unique. Plotting out the journey with the family you work for takes serious consideration and thought. Understanding why periodic reviews are essential is the first step. Frequently, even with safeguards in place, it falls on you to be sure this happens. Don't be afraid to take the initiative and give a gentle reminder.

Why Reviews are Important

Reviews, whether they happen annually or more often throughout the year, have three critical factors: reviews provide both you and the parents with feedback about the job, reviews give you the ability to set and review goals, and reviews are a steppingstone in your professional growth. Each is a significant factor.

Chapter 8. Your Review

Feedback is always helpful. Feedback lets you know how you are doing in your job. Identifying where you excel or need improvement allows you to make changes according to the parent's needs. Feedback is a two-way street. You probably expect your employer to provide reviews with an assessment of your performance on the job, but it's equally important to give the parent your viewpoint of how the job is going, along with areas you would like to discuss. Feedback should also match the expectations outlined in the work agreement. Evaluation of performance cannot be made about an issue to which neither parent or nanny has not already agreed. Think of it this way—if you never agreed either in your work agreement or later verbally to regularly vacuum the family room, it follows that the parent should not be giving you feedback relating to vacuuming the family room.

Setting goals in a nanny position is a way to set out the markers for achievement. If you don't know where you are going, how will you know when you've arrived? Goal setting can be done within the review process with the parent as a team approach.

Make sure that goals align with the job description. If they don't, either the goal needs to be modified or the work agreement requires adjustment. Such adjustments are common as children mature and families shift their priorities.

Nanny Basics and Beyond

Once goals are set—for example, starting biweekly trips to the library to choose books— they should be looked at during future reviews. The goal may then be adjusted at a future date. Goal setting can also bring out new areas to discuss regarding your work agreement, which may consist of new tasks or discontinuing other tasks which then better align with the goals that you and the parent have as partners.

Professional growth is a personal goal that you should strive for throughout your career. Knowledge is power. Knowing your strengths, being aware of areas for improvement, and seeking to increase your knowledge base is empowering. Reviews can help a nanny refocus on the reasons that brought you into this career in the first place and redirect your sight on the children in your care each day. Additionally, reviews can help establish a plan to build skills and expand your proficiency. This factor in the annual review is entirely in the hands of you to expand and develop.

Review in Writing

Memory is an unpredictable thing. With your work agreement as a guide, you may believe that you and your employers will recall with perfect clarity all the details you've discussed, but there will likely be many items that each of you recall differently. Having your review written down will eliminate the need to remember. It will be there to use as a guide for future reviews and as a complementary document to your work agreement.

Additionally, written reviews have value beyond your current position. Your written review can come into play if, for any reason, you don't have a written recommendation letter from an employer. Perhaps the job ended poorly, or the parents are concerned about privacy and they object or refuse to provide you with a reference. You will have the written reviews that attest to the assessment of your performance during your time with the family. A written review provides documentation and a professional snapshot of that job.

The review can be formal or informal. Whether you use a review form that you and the family complete together or you prefer to take more informal notes during your meeting with them, everyone should have a copy for future reference. Nanny Coaching Team has an online review form available for this purpose, and there are other forms and templates available on the internet.

Part-Time or Temporary Positions

Many nannies will work one or more part-time position during the length of their career. They may also take temporary positions to fill periods of time between jobs or to earn additional income.

Permanent part-time positions should be viewed and managed as a full-time position with periodic written reviews. Again, the value of these reviews is in feedback, goal setting, and professional development, as well as with an eye to future employment. Having a review for a more extended temporary position is a good idea. Let's say you took a temporary job for three months working 35 hours a week for a family. Toward the end of this situation, ask for a written performance review along with a letter of recommendation. Both of these documents will serve you well when looking for that next great opportunity.

Short-term temporary jobs, those under three months, may not be candidates for a review but are certainly appropriate for a letter of recommendation. Likewise, long-term "babysitting" positions have value on your résumé, so asking for a letter of recommendation or even a performance assessment from these families can be helpful to you in the future.

The Review Document

Your work agreement is the basis of building the review document. The job duties and expectations found in the work agreement are the foundation of the review document. Remember, the review document should allow for assessment of current job duties, used to set goals, and be available to review previous goals. The document can be used as a self-assessment review for the nanny, which can be shared with the parent during the review conversation or kept for personal use and consideration. If a less formal document is chosen, notes can be substituted but should still include the job duties and expectations. Like the work agreement, the review is a living document, which means that it will change and adapt to reflect the changes in the family, the children, and the position as a whole.

Highlight Areas

All review documents should have the following highlighted areas included in them. However, you may find that some positions require additional items. The work agreement is always the reference point for what to add.

- Duties pertaining to the children—their physical care, activities, outings, meals, laundry, schedule, etc.—should be listed. Provide as much detail as you find in the work agreement—remember they are partner documents.

- Duties pertaining to the household— cleaning or maintenance, family meals, laundry other than the children's, etc.— will be listed.

- Work habits such as communication punctuality, flexibility, professionalism, and other specific markers in the employer-employee relationship should be included. These may not be specifically listed in the work agreement but instead implied.

- Duties beyond the home, which might include errands, groceries, appointments, and other child- and family-related items.

While many of these items can be assessed objectively, others are subjective. You may feel that you perform household duties to a high degree, while the parent may not agree. It might be that she is not fully cognizant of what you do on a daily basis simply because she arrives home after a full day and has her mind on other things. This is where having an opportunity to do a self-assessment may help the parent see the bigger picture that she was unaware of as she shifted from her work to home mode.

Assessment Options

There are three basic types of assessment styles: scale assessment, open assessment, or a mixed assessment. No assessment type is better than another. Instead, you are looking for the method that works best for you and the parent.

The scale assessment is a rating scale with an assigned number. Having the scale of one to five, with one being poor and five being exceptional, allows for a full range of options along with middle ground of three in this case. Contrast this with a scale of one to ten, which has more variables and can have too many options from which individuals can choose.

Scale assessment statements need to be written in a way that is clear and understandable.

An open assessment has no scale or number assignments, but rather a space for writing strengths and areas for improvement. This method allows for details and thoughtful feedback. This type of assessment takes longer to complete, and for some people that is a negative; however, you may get more information from this type of method.

As you have probably guessed, a mixed assessment is a blending of the open and scale types. It could be that some areas are assessed on a scale, and others benefit from the open method. In a truly mixed assessment, you'll see each area rated on a scale, notes on strength in that area and areas for improvement noted, along with a space to set up goals toward which you will work.

Regardless of the type of assessment or review document method, it's vital that you develop a system that works for everyone.

Review more than Annually

> "Take care not to let this slide. It's easy to become comfortable with the way things are up to the point when issues start to creep in. This might result in a great job souring because everyone neglected the importance of the annual review." Becky Kavanagh

Nanny Basics and Beyond

We often think of the performance review on an annual basis, but there are benefits to discussing the job more often. When you begin a position, you might consider a three-month, six-month, and one-year review schedule. You can add more reviews throughout the year, but this is an excellent place to start. As you move into the second year of your position, you can continue the yearly review with additional, and maybe more informal, check-in meetings throughout the year.

Timing is Everything

Typically, the annual review comes on the anniversary of the start date of your position with the family. However, you can certainly set the review for a date before that anniversary date or even shortly after it. Choose a date and time that's convenient for everyone. This may require schedule adjustments to make this happen. Time and location choice are important, as you want this meeting to be you and your employer only, with no children around. Even if you've scheduled it in the evening when children are in bed, it can be a distraction for everyone to be meeting in the parents' home.

"Have this conversation away from the parents' home. It will help everyone to focus on the discussion and planning."
Becky Kavanagh

Chapter 8. Your Review

We all know that having any kind of conversation around children is next to impossible. This particular conversation should really not be around children. Finding an outside location and a babysitter or family member to watch the children for a little while is really important.

Additionally, if you work for two parents, they should both be present if at all possible. Lobby for this as much as you can. If that isn't possible, be sure that you are meeting with the parent who has the most contact with you, and who can make decisions regarding your employment.

Using the technology of face-to-face virtual calls can help alleviate some of these problems. It means that when parents work long hours or travel a lot, they can still virtually connect with you. It also means that you can more easily find a child-free time and -space to talk.

Regardless of when and where you schedule the review, you'll want to remove as many distractions as possible. Phones, TVs, and other distractions should be turned off or on silent and out of sight. Your work agreement comes to the meeting along with your review documents or notes. As nerve-wracking as this may be, try to find a spot where everyone is physically comfortable.

Link to Work Agreement

The work agreement is at this meeting because it has an active role to play. It's the foundation document of your employment, so it makes sense that the work agreement plays its part in the review. As you talk through the review items, look for anything that you'll want to change in conjunction with the work agreement.

The annual review is a combination of performance review or assessment as well as a review of the work agreement, and it can also be the occasion for negotiating your continued employment. This means talking about compensation and other aspects of the agreement. If your performance review is overwhelmingly positive, this gives you more confidence in discussing a raise or increase in benefits going forward. If there are several areas for improvement noted, consider these as opportunities to set strong goals; this should in no way deter you from talking about raises or benefits.

Further Tips

Bring personal notes with you. Many nannies feel nervous or even intimidated in meeting with a parent. Even when you have a close relationship with your employer, this meeting feels different. Having your notes to refer to will boost your confidence and give you a place to look during this face-to-face meeting.

Chapter 8. Your Review

Bring your self-assessment with you if you have completed one. Like your notes, it will provide you with a reference to your discussion and give you a place to look.

Actively listen to the conversation and take notes if it helps you. It is easy to get into a habit of thinking of the next thing we want to say, which can obscure the conversation taking place and may mean you miss something vital that your employer asks or says. Pay attention. Making a note can help you concentrate, but don't let notetaking become its own distraction.

Everyone is probably nervous. Yes, everyone. Even though the parent may be in an authoritative position in her career, she may not take this role when talking with you. The nanny-family relationship and work arrangement are very different from other work situations. This is her home and her children. You have a role that's very personal in her life. No wonder everyone is a bit nervous.

Don't feel pressured. You may be asked to decide on changes to your workload, job expectations, or compensation package that come as a surprise to you. You should never feel pressured to respond immediately. It may be wise to let your employer know that you'd like to think it all over and answer her at a future date. Make sure that you set that deadline with her and then respond on time. Likewise, you may make a suggestion or offer an option to her that she will need to consider. It's respectful and appropriate to give each other space to think things through.

Be proactive. You don't need to wait until your employer brings up the subject of a review. In fact, for some, if you wait for the employer, you'll be waiting a long time. Instead, be proactive and request to get a meeting on the calendar. You may need to be persistent, but do so without becoming angry. While you may be frustrated, consider the view from the parent's side.

The review is important for evaluating performance, setting job and professional goals, and has value beyond your current position. All review documents or notes should be a reflection of your work agreement and be in writing for everyone's benefit. Both you and the family should have a copy of the work agreement and the review documents. Consider that the performance review is different from an annual work review, with updates that reflect job changes as needed. The work agreement needs to be reviewed whenever a performance review is instituted.

BECKY KAVANAGH

Becky Kavanagh has 35 years in the early childhood education field and has been in the nanny industry since 1990. She has an AA degree in Early Childhood Education and a specialty certification in infant and toddler care. In 1998, she was honored by *Parents* magazine for outstanding achievement in the childcare field. Becky is an International Nanny Association (INA) Credentialed Nanny and received the Nanny of the Year honor from INA in 2006. In 2010, she became a certified parent coach and started Heartfelt Parent Coaching to help families and nannies increase their confidence and skills.

Giving back to the industry is important to her. Becky has served on the board of her local nanny support group for many years, and has served on the board of INA for several years. She has been a speaker at industry conferences and nanny training days, as well as early childhood conferences. She joined Nanny Coaching Team at its inception, providing website design and maintenance, technical support, social media marketing, along with being a guest coach. Becky is also the founder and owner of Busy B Services, which provides web, social media, and technical support for solo entrepreneurs so they can focus on their priorities.

HeartfeltParentCoaching.wordpress.com
BusyBServices.wordpress.com

Nanny Basics and Beyond

SECTION II: DEVELOPING YOURSELF

Nanny Basics and Beyond

Chapter 9. Standing Out as a Professional

"Standing out as a professional means that whatever educational level you are at now, you are working to improve your knowledge and skills moving forward." Angela Riggs

I asked Angela Riggs, the former Director of the Early Childhood Education Department at Sullivan University on the Louisville, Kentucky, campus, to share her thoughts with me.

The term you use to describe your position not only influences the way you feel about yourself but how others see you as well. Words like "babysitter" versus "nanny" can seem to diminish your appearance to the world. Many nannies want to add the word "professional" to the career title, in an effort to compel people to take them seriously, but what does it truly mean to be a "professional" nanny?

Whether you are just starting in this industry or have been a nanny for many years, there are a number of characteristics that will help you stand out from the crowd and to which we should all aspire. Equally, there are certain activities that are considered unprofessional to employers, others in the industry, and those outside the industry.

Don't

Poor social media choices top the list. In this day and age, you should understand that everything you put online will eventually make it to someone you don't want to see it. So the best practice is to imagine a future employer will see every post or image that you share. Ask yourself if that is the first impression you want anyone to have of you.

Maintaining healthy boundaries with your employer and the children can also be a challenge. Crossing those boundaries in your relationships with the children can cause friction in your connection with the parents. It is also easy to cross that line with the parents, becoming too close or friendly with one or both of them. This boundary needs to be kept in constant check to ensure professionalism is still in place.

Chapter 9. Standing Out as a Professional

Don't speak ill of your employer or the children to others. While you should find and maintain relationships with friends and mentors, it is far too easy to start "venting" and end up blurting out confidential details about your employer or even the children that you should not be sharing. It is particularly a problem when interacting online or through social media because those details are visible and shareable to the rest of the world.

Failing to follow through on promises or agreements make you look unprofessional. While there are times that you need to get out of an agreement for your health and safety, you should work hard to hold to promises that you make to the parent and the children. If you are frequently late or absent from work, this will be seen as incompetence, and you will likely lose your job. In addition, if you are inefficient or disorganized, you will find it hard to keep any position for long.

How You Act Toward Education

You should strive to be educated in child development and developmentally appropriate practices. While getting a credential, certification, Associate's degree, Bachelor's degree or even a Master's in a field related to the care of children is encouraged, to be a professional nanny, this is not required. But, being a professional nanny means that you are always willing to learn something new. It means that you realize that even if you have been a nanny for 40 years, there is still more to learn.

This continued education can come in many forms. It may be from extensive reading about new scientific studies or behavioral techniques. The knowledge might come from local, national, or international conferences. It might come from online training that benefits you or the family for which you work. Alternatively, it could come from a formal college or university. Whatever path you take to expand your understanding of child development, psychology, health, and safety, is up to you. However, if you want to stand out as a professional, you must continue to learn.

How You Act Toward Children

"A professional nanny puts the needs of the child at the forefront of decisions and plans." Angela Riggs

Putting the needs of the children at the forefront means that you should make on-the-job decisions day to day that ensure the children stay safe and healthy. It also means that you should consider the children in your personal choices as your decisions pertain to your job. As a professional nanny, you should think about how your actions outside of work hours might affect your career and the children for whom you care.

It may be obvious that you should keep the children safe and healthy, but as a professional nanny, you should focus on the whole child. Look for the underlying reasons for negative behavior. Seek a better understanding of the particular struggles through which the children in your care are going. Work to make sure the bond the children have with their parents is as secure as it can be. As a professional nanny, this should not merely be a job but your calling to help raise well-balanced children who will become productive citizens of our world.

As a professional nanny, you should have a basic understanding of developmentally appropriate behaviors and practices for children. It is always important to treat all children as the unique individuals they are; however, it is essential to have a basic understanding of what typical behavior means for a child that age. This can come from experience, but you should also have research to back up your philosophies. A parent might ask and rely on you to help him understand his child. You can go that extra step to research struggles and issues with which the children in your care are coping. This is an excellent opportunity for you to expand your knowledge but also to show the parent how seriously you take your career.

As a professional nanny, you should know that when working with children it is best to be proactive rather than reactive. Setting firm boundaries and enforcing those boundaries with compassion, empathy, and love, is key. Children learn about life and love through fun. You will need to have enough of both with the children in your care. To keep the children healthy and safe, you also need to manage the expectations and behaviors within the house. Finding the right balance of fun and rules can be challenging to master. Learning to balance this often comes with time on the job, but be sure to make these rules and boundaries clear from the beginning. As a professional nanny, you should also follow healthy practices for guiding the behavior of children.

"You are role models for the children in your care. The best way to teach a lesson is to model it. Therefore, you should act and react in the way that will best illustrate positive behaviors to the children in your care." Angela Riggs

How You Act Toward Your Employers
Working as a professional nanny also means that you strictly adhere to a work agreement set up at the time of your employment. Know the value of this document and that it is vital to a successful working relationship with your employer. Having a work agreement not only means that the parent

guarantees certain things to you but that you agree to certain things. A professional nanny does not break this promise.

Offering to sign a confidentiality agreement in addition to your work agreement (or within it) will set you apart from others. It will establish clear boundaries and expectations for sharing information. It guards the privacy of the family, children, home, and you; therefore, the confidentiality agreement shows the parent that you know that your number one job is to ensure the health and safety of his children. Even if confidentiality is not part of your work agreement, you should uphold it.

As a nanny, you are often called on to be flexible with any number of tasks within the job. From the hours worked to schedules of the children, flexibility is an integral part of the job. As a professional nanny, you should navigate these unexpected changes with grace and understanding. However, you should also be clear on your boundaries when it comes to flexibility. It is crucial to be up front about what extra responsibilities or hours you will or will not take on. That being said, a big benefit for most families when having a nanny is the added flexibility and the mindset of teamwork. Standing out from the rest by making your boundaries clear, if done with the respect for the parents, can make you an invaluable asset to the family.

It is always necessary to have appropriate attire to wear to work. Each family's expectations are different, but, as a professional nanny, you need to show respect for your employer by dressing in attire that is not only appropriate for the day's activities but also reflects positively on the family. Wear neat and clean clothing that is easy to move in and is conservative in body coverage. You need to respect any specific dress code the parent has for you.

As a professional nanny, you need to strive to have clear and honest communication with the parents with whom you are employed. No communication will be perfect, but to stand out you need to find healthy and helpful ways to work as a team with your employer.

Above all else you need to follow up on promises, whether these promises involve the work agreement or a commitment made to the children. Integrity is a powerful attribute of the professional nanny.

How You Act Toward Yourself

There are several things you need to be sure you are doing for yourself as a professional nanny. The first is to follow the INA's Recommended Practices for Nannies. This is a list of industry standards that helps elevate the entire in-home childcare industry. Professional nannies should unite to prove the importance of what we do. This list can be found at nanny.org.

Chapter 9. Standing Out as a Professional

You should become involved in professional organizations, both locally and worldwide. The benefits that come from getting to know other like-minded individuals in the same career as you is truly invaluable.

Save your money and income wisely. No nanny job is 100 percent secure. It is more common than you think to lose a job that you thought you would have for many years, so you need to properly manage your wage and resources. Having savings that you can fall back on if the job suddenly ends is important. And, you certainly don't want to find yourself in an unsafe or unhealthy situation but be unable to leave because you cannot afford to lose your job.

As a nanny, you may tend to have the personality that will take care of others before taking care of yourself. While it is undoubtedly important to take care of others, it is equally important to care of yourself. Maintaining your health and well-being is crucial if you are going to take care of children. The job can be stressful at times, and the more hours you work, the more you need to be sure to take time to care for yourself.

Above all else, you need to take pride in what you do and how you act. Let it sink in that you are helping to raise the next generation. The children in your care may go on to be future presidents or professors. They may discover the cure to cancer or win an award for a performance. Caring for this generation is not to be minimized, it should be commended.

Overcoming The Past

Maybe after reading through this chapter, you find yourself feeling that you have made many mistakes in the past. You worry that you will never be a "professional nanny." I am here to tell you that we have all made mistakes. No one is perfect, but the good thing is that you now know the steps that you need to take to improve. You are ready to make positive changes that will move you forward.

If you have made mistakes in the past or been labeled as "unprofessional" and you are ready to make changes, the first step is to be honest. Give full disclosure and be as transparent as you can be as you move forward. You want to get in front of the story with prospective employers and placement agencies, explaining your previous actions but not making excuses for them. You want to emphasize the changes you have made and why you have made them. Then you want to demonstrate through your actions that you are going to rebuild your professional image.

ANGELA RIGGS

Angela Riggs, Quality Enhancement Plan Coordinator at Sullivan University in Kentucky where she supports over 4000 students and dozens of faculty to implement activities and assessments at 4 campuses and 2 learning centers.

Mrs. Riggs has been employed by Sullivan University for the past 19 years. For 16 years, she led the Early Childhood Education Department as the Director/Dean. During that time she built curriculum and a team of educators that prepared professional nannies and early childhood professionals. Her passions include teaching courses in the areas of child development, children's literature, special needs, health and safety and professional development topics with an emphasis on best practices when working with children and families.

Before coming to Sullivan, she was an elementary teacher in Kentucky. Her educational credentials include a master's degree from the University of Louisville, where she specialized in early education and focused on mathematics. Her teaching experience spans preschool to undergraduate-level courses. Other experience includes Department chair of Budget and Professional Development Committees, creating and delivering in-service trainings for teachers developing writing and math portfolios, open-ended question development/trainings, KY Governor's Work Group for Professional Development Standards, online course development and various trainings, Level 5 Trainer for Kentucky, advisory board member for Bright Horizon, Sullivan Active Learning Training Team Leader, NAEYC member, INA member, and past INA elected Board of Directors and Education Committee Chair.

Her new venture is Personalized Education Adventures, where special needs children and families have an educational travel adventure of a lifetime.

PEDAdventures.com

Chapter 10. Healthy Communication

"Consider every conversation as a way to build teamwork with your employers, rather than a problem that you want to complain about." Rachel Lawrence

To understand communication from all angles, I talked with Rachel Lawrence of Morningside Nannies. As a former nanny, current nanny employer, and professional who works to place nannies, Rachel has seen good and bad communication from all angles.

It is often said that communication is the cornerstone of a healthy relationship. This is never truer than it is in the nanny-parent relationship. Every relationship will look different, but you need to be able to find a way to discuss the important and not-so-important

163

events within the family. Building a system that works for both you and the parent from the very beginning will solve a lot of problems down the road, and might mean that you can navigate difficult topics without stress.

> "Open communication means that you are working together for a common goal." Rachel Lawrence.

In the case of your nanny-parent relationship, that goal should be to raise healthy and well-balanced children who will become productive citizens of the world. This common goal should be discussed frequently between you and your employer to help you remember the reason you are working together, especially when you discuss difficult and perhaps heated topics.

Excellent communication with anyone, especially your employer, should come from a place of mutual respect. If you don't respect your employer, you will quickly jump to conclusions about his action or inaction and always assume the worst. If you don't feel that he respects you, you will soon feel used and pushed around. The relationship will be strained, and it will be tough to want to stay to work it out.

Honesty Is Key

Good communication should also come from a place of total honesty. That honesty should be stated in a kind and compassionate manner from both sides, but if the employer begins hiding things from you, the relationship is already broken. The same is true for you. If you are not honest with your experiences throughout the day with the children as well as your perceptions about what is happening, your employer will soon feel that there is something you are hiding and become secretive as well.

A Little Appreciation Goes a Long Way

When communication is right, there is a mutual appreciation for both sides of the situation. You can feel it right away when your employers do not appreciate the work that you do. This can lead to feelings of resentment. You need to show appreciation toward your employers. A little thankfulness can go a long way toward expressing respect for the opportunity to work for their family.

Have a Collaborative Attitude

"When issues arise, both parties need to want to seek a solution."
Rachel Lawrence

For a working relationship to be healthy, there needs to be teamwork. Without that desire coming from both parties, there will be discord. If one party is always getting his way, then the other party will feel resentful. But if both parties have a desire to find a solution, a solution will almost always be found.

Nanny Basics and Beyond

See the Other Party's Perspective
Understanding the different roles each of you plays in the lives of the children and within the home is another critical piece of this puzzle. You should always recognize that the bond the children have with their parent is crucial to the children's development. Your employer should understand and not be threatened by the healthy relationship that you form with the children, because that too is essential to the children's well-being. Both parties should work to see every situation that arises from the other person's point of view.

These topics help you build a foundation for excellent communication with your employer, but I also want to share specific techniques you can use to communicate both daily needs and long-term plans with your employers. There is no one "right" way to communicate. Each employer and each nanny will have their preferred method, but both will need to learn to bend a little to find what works for the whole group.

Face to Face
While there is no "right" method of communication, every effective nanny-employer relationship will need to have face-to-face conversations. Setting up a system where you can speak directly to your employer about the concerns you have is very important. This can be a challenge because, most of the time, you

166

will not want to discuss these sensitive matters with the children around. The good news is that in this technology-based world, there are ways to talk face-to-face without being in physical proximity to each other. Video chat can not only eliminate the chance that "little" ears will overhear things they should not but it can mean you are able to communicate face-to-face even with a parent who travels. Setting up regular video conferences with your employer can keep everyone on the same page and moving in the same direction. However, if it is possible and both parties prefer this method, a physical meeting set up on a monthly or bi-monthly basis can be helpful in developing a successful professional relationship.

Nanny Log

Employers have different expectations for daily communication, but for the sake of your career and peace of mind, nannies should keep a daily log. This can range in detail from merely logging the hours you worked on one end to providing an account for every hour in the children's day and anywhere in between.

Logging your daily hours is vital because it ensures that you and your employer are not just relying on your memory when it comes to getting paid for the time you worked. Even nannies who have guaranteed hours should record the actual hours worked each week.

Nanny Basics and Beyond

A basic outline of what activities the children did on a day-to-day basis is essential. For young children, a parent might want to know when and what they ate so that if something happens when you are not there, written notes can help the parent understand what might have caused the problem. A parent usually wants to have a basic understanding of what older children have done throughout the day. A parent might want you to go a step further and give a running timeline of events in the day. You should be respectful and provide as much or as little detail to help relieve the stress that the parent feels at being away from the children.

Daily logs can be kept in a hand-written form like a notebook or journal that is kept in the home, or they can be kept electronically. Talk to your employer to find the best solution for everyone. If you are not tech savvy but your employer would prefer that you use a digital method, you are going to need to become familiar with this method. There are hundreds of programs and apps that can work, and usually there are tutorials that you can find to help you learn about them.

If you hate writing out notes by hand, but your employer prefers to use this method, then you will need to learn to adjust. Perhaps a good solution to this problem is to have you use an app or program that will allow you to print out the log at the end of the day so that you can still work digitally but your employer can have a physical document to hold.

Scheduling

From the hours that you work to the activities that the children participate in, scheduling can be a source of great miscommunication. There are many methods that you and your employer can use to keep this from becoming a problem. Apps for the phone and computer can be an easy way that everyone can look at and make needed changes to schedules. This is especially helpful for families who change the nanny's hours often or whose children have a lot of activities. Be sure to look at this daily. Both parties should get into the habit if possible to notify the others when there are changes.

In-The-Moment Issues

There will be times when you need to contact your employer during the workday. How you go about doing this will depend on the job your employer has and what method he would prefer that you use.

Texts or messaging is a standard method used today by many families. A parent may ask for pictures and updates to see what is going on at home. Often the parent will want to text and check in with you throughout the day, just to touch base. You should not jump to the conclusion that this means the parent does not trust you. Sometimes a parent just wants to continue to be a part of his child's day. Other parents do not want to be interrupted at work unless there is an emergency. Respect the parent's wishes.

It is also important to discuss how the parent would like you to communicate more significant behaviors from the children that can come up on any given day. Does he want an immediate message sent to him or would he wish to be told at the end of the day? What about emergencies?

It is also helpful for you to know how you will be informed if there are job expectations that you are not meeting. Will the parent share these details in a message or will he request a face-to-face? Conversely, if you have an issue with a request or expectation, does the parent want that comment in an email, in the daily log, or via another form of communication? These conversations are best done away from little ears, but they will need to be thought out to ensure both parties know what to do when they happen. In chapters 11 and 12 we will discuss why it is so important to address these concerns right away and not let them linger.

Nanny Cameras

Nanny cameras, "nanny cams," used to be a tool that the very wealthy used in secret, but these days they are pretty commonplace in almost every nanny household. Ethically, a family should inform you if you are being recorded or even if there is a live video feed. However, different states have different laws and not all protect the nanny from hidden cameras. A nanny should always assume that she is being watched.

A nanny cam is not necessarily bad. It can work to improve the relationship and communication that you have with your employer, but a nanny cam's use needs to be coupled with the aspects of open communication discussed at the beginning of the chapter. Nanny cams can help the parent be involved in the lives of his children and it can help him see you are a fantastic caregiver. It can also help you and the parent stay on the same page, because the parent can see how you handled a situation so that he can handle it in the same way.

Dealing with the Tough Subjects

As a nurturer, you may have trouble approaching the tough topics with your employer. It can seem overwhelming to talk to your employer about an issue that you want resolved. However, here are several tools to help you step up and speak out.

Always start a conversation on a positive note. Maybe there was a moment you witnessed with the children that was particularly moving, or perhaps you can share a positive aspect of the relationship you have with your employer. It could even be an action you observed the parent do that was helpful to children.

Starting the conversation with a genuine compliment to the parent can set the tone for the rest of the discussion.

State the matter, remembering to display a collaborative attitude: you are looking for a solution rather than you feel your employer has done something wrong. Using "I" statements rather than "you" statements can help avoid a defensive response. Statements that start with phrases like "I have been noticing," or "I see that you would like me to" will show the parent that you are open to changing the way you do things to find a solution. That willingness to give a little will go a long way in resolving the problem.

Finally, conclude your statement with another compliment about the parent or child. This leaves the parent feeling that you respect and understand the family. In the next few chapters we will discuss a bit more about being assertive and conflict resolution.

Parents Who Don't Communicate Well

Many times, the breakdown in communication is not because you are timid but because you work for a parent who does not communicate well. There are many reasons this might happen, and here are several potential solutions to the problem.

Make a note of the place, tone, and timing of any negative statements. If the parent tends to come home and share negative feedback to you or no feedback at all, consider what the reason behind that behavior might be. This is especially true if this behavior is out of character or infrequent. Even frequent and common behaviors likely have an underlying cause. Perhaps events at work are causing stress. Maybe the parent has something more he needs you to do but is unable to express what that "something more" is.

Before you react, it is best to assess the full situation, or at least as much of it as you know. Addressing the negativity at that moment is usually not the best thing to do because you will be emotional and your words might come out wrong. You should be careful to not agree to anything that you are unwilling to do, but there is nothing wrong with saying "I need to consider that." Often when presented with a question or statement, people feel that they need to answer right away, but sometimes silence is helpful. Take a step back so you can see the situation differently, and then find a different way to respond.

By waiting to respond until you have a better idea of what you want to say, you have a better chance of being heard. A long pause gives the parent an opportunity to re-examine his words and actions too. And it brings attention to the discussion in a way that cannot be equaled with volume or tone.

In moments of friction, do not take the parent's initial response personally. As I said before, your employer's reaction often comes from a place outside of your control and may not even really be about you but the parent's other experiences in the day. We all tend to take our frustration out on those we are close to, and this often is what parents do. Look at the root of the response and the sources of the frustration. Realize that once emotions have settled, you can work with this person to create a better atmosphere for work and for the children.

If this type of situation comes up over and over again, you will want to ask yourself a few questions. The first is if you want to work in this type of situation. You might want to try to communicate through a third party to see if the issues can be resolved with the help of someone not emotionally attached to the situation. If the job was found through a placement agency, asking its staff for help is the ideal choice. In fact, many high-quality agencies offer this service to parents. If you found your job in another manner, you could try working with a life or nanny coach. Often these people can help you work through the roadblocks to come to mutual understanding and find a solution.

If the situation is getting no better, despite your continued efforts to find positive solutions, it might be time to leave the position. Remember that you cannot fix everything and that you need to take care of yourself. You should not feel guilty about leaving a situation that you believe is not good for your emotional health.

As we wrap up this topic, I just wanted to remind you that communication is often overlooked in the nanny job, but it is the foundation on which the position will stand. It takes effort and patience, but even lousy communication can be turned around and become a positive situation.

RACHEL LAWRENCE

Rachel Lawrence has over 15 years of experience working in all facets of the in-home childcare industry. Rachel has worked as a household manager and nanny for charges from birth to 8 years old. She operated her own nanny placement agency, and was awarded the Young Entrepreneur of the Year 2008 Award for her commitment to excellence and innovation by a partnership of regional and national Small Business Associations. Rachel also served as the Operations Manager for the International Nanny Association, running daily operations as well as planning and implementation of its annual conference. Currently, Rachel works as the Placement Specialist for Morningside Nannies in Houston, Texas, and, as a working mom, she is also a nanny employer.

Rachel is a big proponent of developing and adhering to high industry standards. She held membership in the International Nanny Association for nearly a decade, and served on its Board of Directors. She also has a long track record of attending and speaking at industry conferences, including those put on by the Association of Premier Nanny Agencies and the International Nanny Association.

When she's not working, Rachel enjoys spending time outdoors with her family, including her three young children—daughter Quinn and boy/girl twins Emery and Grey.

MorningsideNannies.com

Chapter 11. Asserting Yourself

"Assertive people state their opinions confidently while being respectful of others." Ryan Jordan

To help me understand this topic I talked with Ryan Jordan of Educated Nannies. As a business owner and mom, Ryan has a positive yet assertive presence in all she does and is able to bring that quality out in others.

It is widely recognized that being assertive is beneficial in any professional relationship. Finding the middle ground between passive behavior and aggressive behavior as a nanny is necessary, but it is far too easy to fall into the old passive-aggressive behavior styles than to be genuinely assertive. Parents have greater respect for you when you are positive, kind, and confident. Plus, they will be more willing to receive information from you if your delivery is factual and free of emotion.

Other Patterns of Behavior

You can be passive when you ignore your own needs out of fear of confrontation or judgment. This means your needs are not being met and issues will not be resolved. It leaves you feeling used and often abused.

Being aggressive means you are forceful in getting your needs met, often ignoring or attacking others' opinions, wants, or even rights. While being aggressive might be effective in caring for yourself, it can alienate other people and leave them fearful of interactions with you.

You can also fall into the passive-aggressive approach. This behavior appears when you do not want to confront others directly, but you do want to meet your needs. Unfortunately, passive-aggressive behavior results in manipulation and quiet hostility.

Passive Nannies on the Job

As a nanny, you work with many different people where you need to find a way to assert yourself without falling into bad habits of being passive, aggressive, or passive-aggressive.

You most likely will work with many placement agencies in your nanny career. Placement agencies know when you are passive because you seem too afraid to ask any follow-up questions or seem too timid to voice your expectations. Placement agencies might be reluctant to place you in a top position because they know you may end up getting lost in the process.

Your employer knows you are passive because you start off the job with almost no concerns or questions about the position. You are willing to do just about anything that is asked of you. Nanny employers will be pretty ready to work with the passive nanny, at least at first. Unfortunately, you cannot stay passive forever. You will burn out, and eventually either snap, becoming aggressive, or have a slow slide into passive-aggression. You may end up burning out and just want to leave suddenly.

Aggressive Nannies on the Job

Agencies know that if you become impatient or commanding in your follow-up emails and phone conversations you may be an aggressive nanny; therefore, it may be challenging to work with you. They would be reluctant to place you in a position because it might be hard for any family to please you completely and the agency may not want to work with you at all.

Your employer sees you as aggressive when almost every concern or question you have is about your own needs. While your employer might want to meet your needs, the needs of her own family take a priority. That employer will be reluctant to work with you because she knows that she will never entirely please you and in trying to she will likely sacrifice her family's security and peace.

Passive-Aggressive Nannies on the Job

If you are passive-aggressive, at first, it can be hard to spot you. Placement agencies often find you more passive at first, with few questions or concerns to discuss. However, when they get to know you a bit more, they may see an underlying hurt or anger that wells up and comes out in manipulation or backbiting. Outwardly, you are pleasant, but behind the scenes, you may be angry and annoyed.

If you are passive-aggressive, like the passive nanny, at first, your employer will love you. She will likely enjoy your outward accommodating attitude and mild demeanor. Unfortunately, most passive-aggressive behavior results in manipulation and gossip. At some point, you will vent your frustration to the wrong person, and that will get back to your employer. Manipulation is another way you will try to meet your needs, and this will, unfortunately, end up backfiring on you. Manipulation only works to dig a hole, a hole you will struggle to get yourself out of.

Assertive Nannies on the Job

When you are assertive, you stand up for your needs and feelings but try not to minimize others' needs.

Placement agencies can tell when you are assertive because you not only carefully try to

Chapter 11. Asserting Yourself

understand the agencies' process but you respond promptly and have a respectful tone when asking questions. It is important to remember that the agency is looking for the best nanny to fit every job and that sometimes that takes time.

When working with a parent, to be assertive, you should approach every situation from the perspective of teamwork, trying to see the parent's point of view. You should not disregard your needs but you should also not overlook the needs of your employer and the children in your care. Therefore, when your needs and their needs are in conflict, thoughtful conversation needs to take place. Do not be afraid to express how a request or comment from your employer affects you, but display your grasp of the full circumstance.

Tips for the Passive Nanny

If you are a passive nanny, you need to work to build up your confidence. When confronted about a problem, repeat the statement that your employer said out loud so that you can fully process it. This also allows your employer to hear what she is asking you to do precisely. If you have been passive for a long time, your employer might just be used to you doing whatever is wanted. By repeating the request back to her, the parent will begin to hear what she has been asking of you.

If you tend toward passive actions, practice "I" statements instead of "you" statements when talking with parents, like "I feel I am not being heard," "I am requesting time off," or "I need to make changes to the work agreement." When preparing to talk with the family, practice these statements so that they roll off your tongue.

Example.

Employer: "I need you to work this weekend."

Nanny: "You are asking me to work this weekend. I feel that might be a challenge because I am feeling drained and was looking forward to the weekend off so that I can give your children my best Monday through Friday."

Passive people are often not confident making decisions and are afraid of making mistakes in life and hurting others. If you are a passive nanny, you need to continually remind yourself that you are worth the time and energy it takes to keep yourself happy and healthy. You matter too.

"Be clear with what you need and want, and then ask for it." Ryan Jordan

As a passive nanny, you need to realize that sometimes meeting your own needs means saying "No, thank you" to requests and carving out time for yourself. On the surface it might not seem like it, but this is better for everyone in the long run.

Tips for the Aggressive Nanny

If you are an aggressive nanny, you tend to focus your own needs first. Ironically, many of the tips for passive nannies can also be helpful for aggressive nannies. Calmly repeating the request back can help the aggressive nanny stop and think about the reason for the request. Using "I" statements can help start the conversation off in a respectful tone.

Example.

Employer: "The dishes were not put away last night."

Nanny: "You are stating that you are upset that the dishes were not entirely put away before I left last night. I understand that is important to you, but because of Molly's extra homework last night, I was just not able to get to them."

Aggressiveness often comes from a place of fear rather than anger or disrespect, but it often sounds to others like you don't care. For this reason, it is important to state your opinion about a matter without emotions attached. This might mean that you do not answer every question right away but that you ask to think about your answer and get back to the other person. It might mean that you need to walk away from a situation for a time until you can come back having considered all the positions.

"Stop and visualize the person that you want to be and how the words that you 'want' to use might sound to others."
Ryan Jordan

Doing this takes practice and patience but it can become second nature, and it does not mean that your needs will not be met. When aggressive nannies work to become the solution to the problem rather than making the problem bigger, everyone wins.

Tips for the Passive-Aggressive Nanny
If you are the passive aggressive nanny, you are likely trying to get the best of both worlds with your good intentions. You are straddling both extremes. You may even be thinking that means you are assertive. However, being passive one moment and aggressive another is not assertive. It is damaging to relationships.

The same tips suggested for passive and aggressive nannies will be useful to you, but you may need to take extra steps to face confrontation in a healthy manner.

Perhaps the best way to explain how you can engage with your employer without falling into your passive-aggressive rut is to give a specific example or two.

Situation A: Parents not paying on time:
- Approach the topic assuming that they are not doing this intentionally.
- State the facts clearly and briefly.

Chapter 11. Asserting Yourself

- Be willing to be a part of the solution.

Nanny: "I feel that there might be a breakdown in the way that my wages are being paid. This is the third time that the check has not been paid by the agreed upon time. I understand that you are so busy with work and that when you get home you want to spend time with the children, but I need to know that I will be paid what was promised, when it was promised. Is there a way I can help find a solution?"

Situation B: Parents who regularly do not arrive home on time:

- Give the parents grace and understanding: you know that they don't want to be at work any longer than they have to and very likely would rather be home with their children.
- Be up front about how this affects you and your life outside of work.
- Be prepared if a permanent solution is not found but be willing to work to find a solution.

Nanny: "I have noticed that this is the fifth time this month that you have been home later than expected. I understand that must be frustrating for you because you crave quality time with your children as much as they want it with you. It is also challenging for me to have a work schedule that might change at the drop of a hat because I need to plan activities outside of work. Do we need to look at my work schedule and adjust it for a later time or is there another solution we can look at to make this work?"

More Tips on Being Assertive

"Never communicate anything important via email or text. Be brave and have a conversation. You cannot control how people react; you can only control how you respond." Ryan Jordan

It is so easy to get out your phone and send a text or email. Maybe you are a person who needs to type or write out your thoughts before you have a conversation, but emails and text messages can be taken the wrong way so very quickly. It is much healthier to have the tough discussions in person or at very least with voice. It takes much longer to send typed messages, and the reality is that you can spend an entire day sending messages back and forth that are misunderstood or you can take 10 minutes to have a conversation.

Many problems start with people who make false assumptions about another person. It is easy to see only what is on the surface, then take that and let your imagination run wild. As an assertive nanny, you need to address the situation for what it is and not to make assumptions about it, Avoid making the judgment until you have all the facts. If you are

Chapter 11. Asserting Yourself

in doubt, then you need to ask follow-up questions out of respect with the goal to understand the situation and the other person more.

Sometimes the best thing you can do is disengage for a while and take a step away from the conversation. Emotions can run high when dealing with your employer's expectations of you or your expectations of your employer. If you find that you are so emotionally charged that you cannot see your employer's point of view, it is time to take a step back, gather your thoughts, and find a better time to talk.

It may sound silly, but one of the best ways to work toward being more assertive is to specifically plan what you will say and then practice it several times. It can even help to think about what your employer's response to each statement might be, so that you can have an idea of what you might say if that is said. This exercise will actually help you see your employer's point of view a bit better as well.

You can ask a friend to help you prepare, or you can do it on your own. Remember though, a little of this goes a long way. There is no need to rehearse hours on hours. Once you have your response to several typical reactions, walk away from it and do something else. Practicing for too long can cause even more stress.

Dealing with an Aggressive Parent

Far too often, nannies are confronted by parents who are aggressive in their interactions. The first step to dealing with an aggressive parent is to recognize the behavior for what it is and to avoid retaliating with aggressive behavior yourself. You should remain calm and avoid getting defensive about the topic. Sometimes it is appropriate to defuse the situation with humor, but that does not always work. Try to read the situation and know your audience.

Take several breaths and step away for a moment if you can. You want your first words to be thoughtful, not reactionary. Use the tools listed above. Repeat the request or accusation and use "I" statements to share your own opinion. If the situation calls for it, accept blame for what you did or could have done better, but don't accept fault if you did nothing wrong.

Move on to providing a potential solution to the problem if you are able. Ultimately you might have to accept that your employer does not like what has happened and that you might not be able to fix it. If the situation is still heated at this point, ask to consider the issue further to decide how you might be able to resolve it. Agree to come back to the problem at a later date.

Remember that you need to surround yourself with positive nannies who are also realistic in their approach to work. You need people in your life who are not going to tell you what you want to hear but will tell you what you need to hear. If you are a passive nanny, you need people encouraging you to stand up for yourself. If you are an aggressive nanny, you need people showing you the other perspective. If you are passive-aggressive, you need people telling you to confront the situation head-on. The nanny industry is unique, and its challenges are complicated by many things. Work to stay as positive as you can in every situation, always looking at it from different points of view.

RYAN JORDAN

Ryan Jordan is the founder and CEO of Educated Nannies in Los Angeles. Ryan has more than 20 years of experience working with children and families as a childcare expert, teacher, nanny, and tutor.

Ryan earned a multiple-subject teaching credential and Master of Arts in Education from Pepperdine University. In addition to teaching, Ryan spent more than six years as a full-time professional nanny for high-profile families in LA. She taught 1st through 4th grades, and has tutored numerous children in literacy, phonemic awareness, math, and ISEE test preparation. Known for her positive attitude and Midwestern work ethic, Ryan took her nickname "The Educated Nanny" and turned it into a thriving business.

Educated Nannies earned the Red Tricycle Award for Most Helpful Childcare Agency in Los

Angeles. Ryan was also featured in *The Huffington Post* for young entrepreneurs who inspire others, and she was nominated for the *Los Angeles Business Journal*'s Women Making a Difference award.

In addition to guiding families in finding childcare, Ryan is the proud mother of a three-year-old son and one-year-old daughter who fill her days with laughter, an abundance of love, and toddler challenges. Ryan's enthusiasm for learning, along with the joy of witnessing a child's "a-ha moments," continues to inspire her today.

EducatedNannies.com

Chapter 12. Dealing with Conflict

"When you take a second to defuse the emotion in the other person, you can both begin to solve the problem in a simple, non-emotional manner."
Tracey Chipps

I talked with Tracey Chipps, a 23-year seasoned professional nanny whose cheery and uplifting presence has always been refreshing to me. Her perspective on conflict resolution is inspiring.

Conflict
The word produces images of arguments, debate, and controversy. Many people avoid conflict at all costs, but should we automatically consider "conflict" a bad thing? Conflict can actually strengthen relationships and build trust. Having disagreements ultimately can show

191

that you value the opinion of the other person and it can be a learning experience for both parties. That is, if it is done respectfully.

Conflict in the Nanny-Parent Relationship

There are many reasons why conflict arises in the relationship you have with your employer. Unfulfilled expectations can cause both parties to be resentful toward the other. You may feel unappreciated in the role you play in the lives of the children for which you care. A parent can become apprehensive about your presence in the home. Sometimes conflict is present right from the start because of an improper match. The critical thing to remember is that peace is possible if both parties are willing to work together.

Don't Let Conflict Linger

"Do not let conflict linger, but instead take the time to work through the painful process of looking for a solution." Tracey Chipps

It is natural to panic and want to flee from conflict. Lots of people do everything they can to avoid it. When conflict arises and one or both parties decide to ignore it or deal with it later, that only works to let the situation grow. When one person in the situation is frustrated about something and it is not dealt with right away, those feelings not only grow stronger but they transfer to other situations.

The conflict might have started when your employer did not back you up with a discipline you gave his children. The next morning you arrive at work with a sink full of dirty dishes. Your mind now lumps both those situations together, and you might even feel that he is intentionally disrespecting you. The one dispute has grown and is beginning to taint all other interactions. You might end up saying something foolish because your mind is equating one action with another. If you don't address the situation, before you know it, every word your employer says to you will be seen through the lens of this one, growing interaction.

That is why it is best to address the issue right away with a calm and straightforward statement so that the problem is out there: "So that you know, I had taken the tablet away from Julie because she refused to clean up her craft supplies when asked. I know you were unaware of that. Can we work out a system where I can better communicate with you when I give her a consequence in the future?"

To deal with the example of the dirty dishes, you could say something like, "This morning I noticed that there were unwashed dishes left in the sink from the night before. I took care of them because I know you must have been busy. I just wanted to remind you that while I want to be able to help the family as much as possible, mornings with the children for me are also busy, and I might not always have time to accomplish that in addition to my other responsibilities."

Temporarily Walk Away

There are times when faced with a particularly frustrating situation that you feel that you are too emotional to interact with your employer at that moment. Alternatively, the children could be present, and you don't want to contradict their parents in front of them. This is a great time to say something like, "I am working to understand your perspective and would like to discuss it further with you soon." Then be sure to follow up quickly.

Analyze Your Thoughts

It might help you to write out the feelings you have about a particular situation before having that conversation with the parent. The act of handwriting or typing your thoughts and what you want to say can be cathartic. It can also help you to clarify your ideas. This is your chance to analyze the situation before you discuss it. There are times when you will feel better after writing the story down. You may even find that it was you who overreacted and you are now willing to let it go. This can the end of that problem, but be careful with it at the same time. It is harder than it seems to let things go. Take the situation with the dishes again. If you don't mind cleaning those dirty dishes in the morning, maybe it is not worth bringing it up in the moment. Perhaps it is just a topic that you jot down to mention the next time you meet face to face with your employer and suggest that dishwashing be something that you add to the work agreement. However, if the issue is one that truly bothers you and you know will continue to bother you if repeated, then saying something soon is the right thing to do.

You will want to pinpoint what the exact problem is and express it in a non-threatening manner. Use phrases like "in my experience," "my understanding is," or "have you considered." Always be specific when discussing events, stating when they happened and what occurred.

Be Ready to Compromise

"Approach conflict with a promise to find a true and helpful solution."
Tracey Chipps

Approaching conflict in this way means you don't assume the parents will be the only ones to make adjustments; you have make it clear that you are willing to compromise too. In the situation with the dishes, you could add, "If not having to worry about the dishes the night before is something that you feel would be valuable to you, we can discuss how this might be added to my work agreement." Back up your suggestions with precise examples, experiences, or articles.

Listen and Defuse

As you get into a discussion with your employer about an issue you do not see eye to eye on, really listen to what he is saying. Look him in the face and watch for clues from him other than his voice. What emotion do you see coming from him as he discusses it?

- Is he angry?
- Is he worried?
- Does he feel disrespected in some way?

Take a second to consider his perspective. What can you say to defuse the intense emotion that he feels?

- Can you say something about the respect you have for him?
- Can you express your understanding that he is worried about his children?
- Do you owe him an apology?

Choosing to stop and listen and then respond based on what you heard will not only help you know what to say, it can help you calm your employer so that you can work out a solution.

Minimizing Conflict

Not all conflict is avoidable; however, here are a few tips that can help minimize conflicts you have with your employers. The first tip is to ask thoughtful questions during the interview, so that you get to know the parent and the whole family. Many times, conflict can be avoided simply by not taking a job with a family that is not a good match with you.

A strong work agreement can eliminate many of the potential issues with the job. Clarifying responsibility and expectations on both sides from the beginning will help make the road smoother down the way.

Having regular face-to-face meetings, at least monthly, with your employer will give both you and him a chance to voice concerns and tweak roles as you go, so that small frustrations do not become big ones. Along these lines, when there are new duties added to your expectations, those should be added to the work agreement right away. If you have agreed to do something in your job, it should be on the work agreement, period.

While it might take courage, it is so much easier to have a conversation about something that is bothering you immediately after it happens than it is to bring it up weeks or months later. Let's look at that issue with the employer who gave the child the tablet after you had taken it away from her. If you don't mention anything to your employer about it, chances are the next time you discipline the child, she will run straight back to her father to have the consequence reversed. This will cause you to be more frustrated every time it happens, not to mention that it undermines the respect the child

Nanny Basics and Beyond

should have for you. So when your next face-to-face comes, it is going to be more difficult for you to address the topic without emotion attached to it. Plus, in this situation, a lot of damage to the relationship you have with the child will be done and will be very hard to reverse. Being honest about the problem right away will mean that you save the healthy connection you have with the child and you don't end up talking with your employer in anger.

Building a True Team

Teams can grow closer together through conflict. If you are in the honeymoon phase of the job, conflicts might be small but the conflicts that you are not dealing with now will become bigger problems later on. Being part of a team means that you work together to figure out how to move forward, with every effort to make everyone happy. Make sure that you use the word "team" right from the first interview. Let your potential employer know that you will give your all to the team and continue to work together for your common goal: raising healthy and well-balanced children who will someday be a productive part of the world.

Another important aspect of teamwork within the relationship of nanny and parent is to make sure you are communicating with both parents when possible. If you are employed in a two- (or more) parent family, you should be having regular face-to-face meetings with all parents. If you are employed by a single parent, but there are other parents not living in the home, usually (but not always) you will still need to include them as part of the team.

Compliments

"Compliments make you feel like you are part of something bigger than yourself. They make you feel like part of the team." Tracey Chipps

Remember to give the parent sincere compliments. You cannot imagine the stress, guilt, and second-guessing that goes into parenting. When parents receive compliments for even the smallest of details, they are going to be so much more willing and able to receive suggestions from you.

Ultimately, this is all about the children, and when parents and nannies work together as a team to overcome conflict and grow closer, the children benefit. They benefit from the positive and uplifting atmosphere that is created, but they also benefit from witnessing what it is like to work together for a common goal. So in this way, conflict really can be a positive thing.

TRACEY CHIPPS

Tracey Chipps is a Professional Teaching Nanny specializing in birth to age 5. She has worked primarily within the Duke University

Hospital family of doctors in Durham, NC. Her areas of expertise fall in Positive Potty Training, Kindergarten Readiness, and creating a sleep-conducive environment for children.

In 2015, Tracey received her 20-year Service Pin Award from the International Nanny Association in Cancun, Mexico. She was also nominated in 2013 for the Spark Award for Excellence in Nanny Care through NannyBizReviews. In 2000, Tracey founded Triangle Area Nanny Group or T.A.N.G. which ran for a successful 13 years. She has hosted two National Nanny Training Day events and continues to mentor nannies new to the profession. She has been trained as a Newborn Care Specialist through Newborn Care Solutions.

Tracey is the owner of Nanny919, LLC, which offers consulting for parents and professional development for nannies. Tracey attends annual nanny conferences to keep on top of trends and growth in the nanny industry. She has been quoted in the Be the Best Nanny Newsletter, local newspapers and is a guest blog writer for Regarding Nannies. She is the proud godmother of her very first charge, who she has watched grow from an adorable 1-year-old into a beautiful young woman. Tracey actively volunteers in her community and is a pit bull lover and advocate. She enjoys cooking, spending time in nature, bicycling, repurposing projects, and travel.

Chapter 13. Self-Care and the Nanny

"Self-care does not need to happen just in your off hours. Self-care should be something that you are engaging in on the job as well." Greta Schraer

To gather a wealth of knowledge about self-care, I talked with Greta Schraer of CincyNanny about this topic. Greta is a busy mom and business owner who knows when to step out in faith and act, and when, for the sake of herself, to say no.

Self-care is a hot topic these days, with self-help books too numerous to count. Many years ago the idea of self-care was foreign. It is only recently that the phrase has caught on. Were generations before us not in need of self-care? Did they not have the same emotional requirements that we do today?

Nanny Basics and Beyond

The reality is that our world has changed dramatically from what it was even 30 years ago. The pace of life is so much faster, so instant, that it is tough to slow down to take care of yourself when you are in the "flow" of the world. When it comes to you, as a nanny, taking care of yourself becomes even more complicated.

The way you care for yourself has a direct impact on the level of care you can give the children. If you are too tired to play with the children, they will notice. If you are exhausted and can't find the patience any longer, that will end up negatively affecting everyone in the house. Your goal should be to find wholeness. That means being physically, emotionally, and spiritually healthy, as well as financially stable and socially balanced.

Isolating

Nanny positions are unique in that they can be very isolating. With many jobs, even other jobs caring for children, individuals have colleagues whom they are around every day. Teachers have other teachers. Nurses usually have other nurses who they interact with throughout the day. However, nannies interact almost exclusively with children (and occasionally another service professional); therefore, it is vital that you find ways to be around other adults.

Strategically planning play dates and getting involved in adult-child classes are good ways to make sure that you are interacting with adults. However, even if you cannot leave the house with the children, you can still become active in local nanny support groups when you are not on the clock. These groups can be especially beneficial for those of you who are homebound. Online groups can be helpful to you if you do not have any local groups.

It is also important to make sure you have a life outside of the nanny world. Engage in the community by volunteering or find a hobby that you love. Don't neglect your own family and friends for the sake of your job. You may feel pushed to work overtime whenever asked and prep activities outside of working hours. While those extra activities can make you stand out as a professional, be careful not to use all your free hours consumed with work thoughts. The only way to be a fantastic nanny who is 100 percent there for the children is to disengage as much as possible when not at work. It is going to keep you healthier in the long run.

No Breaks

Another part of the nanny job that is unique and may cause you to burn out is that most of you have no real breaks during your workday. Nannies typically work from 8 to 12 hours a day, and unless the children are in school and you are not in charge of the management of the home, you need to be "on" during that entire time. This can be exhausting.

It is important to build habits into your day that keep you focused on doing things that you enjoy too. Maybe that means putting the children in a stroller for a 30-minute walk every day or doing yoga with them. Maybe you love to color; you could bring several grown-up coloring books and markers to use while the children are coloring in their own books. If your little ones nap, you may get a break at least from the "childcare" part of the job, but we all know that there is so much to do during that time.

Find ways to make it fun for yourself. If parents allow it, plan a phone call with a friend every day during nap time or save your lunch until a peaceful moment while the children nap and take 30 minutes to enjoy calm while you eat. If the family has a home gym, find out if you can use it to keep your body healthy too. Experiment with different ideas as you work to keep yourself from going crazy during long days, but always keep the parent you work for informed of your plans.

Service Mindset

"It is so important that you stop putting yourself last on the to-do list and start thinking about what you need to do to care for yourself." Greta Schraer

As a member of the service industry, you likely have a service mindset when it comes to other people. You are the first to say you can help out; you are willing to stay late and arrive early. You are always thinking of the needs of others and very often forget that you have needs as well.

There is a reason that every time you are on a plane, the flight attendants announce: "In the event of an emergency, the oxygen mask will deploy. Passengers traveling with those needing assistance should put their own mask on before assisting others." To a nanny, this seems crazy. It is your job to keep the little ones safe. If they need oxygen, it is your job to get them oxygen. You forget so easily that unless *you* are getting oxygen, you won't be able to help anyone else. If you keep going at the pace of insanity, helping everyone else, before you know it, you will pass out because you forgot all about yourself.

Care for the Home

Most nannies do home care in addition to childcare to at least some degree. Even if it just means that you are picking up the toys with the children, you are responsible for part of the upkeep of the home. Do you spend so much time cleaning and organizing the home you work in that you begin to neglect your own home? This is a common problem in many careers. What is that old saying that a carpenter's house is never done? When you spend your days doing laundry and dishes at work, the last thing you want to do is go home and do the same there.

You can get creative with this. Perhaps you have a roommate or partner at home with whom you can negotiate so that you have less of the responsibility for these activities. Maybe you can talk to your employers about doing your laundry at their house since you are there so much of the time. Think outside the box and find ways to make it work.

Long Days

If you are one of the nannies who work 12 or more hours a day for four days a week or more, I am talking to you about this next point. This includes those of you who take on side jobs on a regular basis. I need you to honestly ask yourself: Is it working for me?

If your honest answer is that it does work for you, excellent. Maybe you have worked out systems and activities throughout the day that help you do the intensive job for those long hours and not feel burned out. Still, I would urge you to keep a close eye on that to make sure it is not getting out of control. Alternatively, maybe these insane hours are temporary, and you have a plan to cut back soon. Perhaps you are a Newborn Care Specialist, travel nanny, or other temporary nanny and you work long shifts for several weeks, and then have off for several weeks. If it works for you, great.

If your answer to my previous question was "I have to do it," "It is what the family needs," "I need the money to pay bills," or "I don't have any options," then read on. You can find options to take care of yourself while working to meet the needs of the family. You can ask the family to hire a nighttime babysitter to care for the children in the evenings. You could request that the parents find a second nanny to cover different days of the week and split the job in half. If part of the problem with the long hours is the commute, consider moving closer to work or even seeing if a live-in position is something the parent would be willing to consider. You have options, but it might mean that you need to get creative. Talk to friends or a nanny coach. Perhaps there are ideas that you have not considered before. If you are working the insane hours because of money, ask yourself if any amount of money is worth your health and well-being.

Blurry Boundaries

This relationship can often become blurry because your employer is also your partner in raising children. Some parents end up wanting the nanny to be more like a friend and confidant than an employee, while others are unwilling to share any details about their personal life with you. You need to reflect on what you want out of the relationship. Maybe you work for a family where one or both of the parents are like your best friend, and you love it. If you are able to navigate the ups and downs that will come with that close of a relationship while that same person pays you, then there is nothing wrong with it. However, you may find that you need to place boundaries on the relationship you have with your employer.

Off-Hours Communication

One of the stumbling blocks that often occur in communication is when the parent continues to reach out to you in your off hours. Just like there are times the parent is at work and you need to get ahold of her for something important, there are times the parent is at home and needs to ask you something. While you might be OK with off-the-clock messaging, this can get out of control. There needs to be a clear path of communication set up for when the parent must ask you something in your off hours.

Text messages seem to be one of the best ways to go in this day when most people have their phone handy. However, it is a good idea to set expectations about the speed at which parents can expect a reply. If you go to bed at 9 PM, make it clear to the parents that you will likely not read a text message after this time of day. If you have activities after work when you will be completely unavailable, share these details with the parents. If you want to be contacted only in the event of an emergency at any non-working point, make it clear that if they reach out to you during this time, you will only respond if available.

Chapter 13. Self-Care and the Nanny

Setting this expectation before contacts get out of control can save time, energy, and conflict in the future.

Overtime

Not all, but most, nannies are willing to work overtime hours. Weeknights or weekends are options that many parents take advantage of, but if you would prefer not to work these extra hours or are finding that "occasionally" has turned into almost every weekend, then you should set boundaries for overtime hours as well.

Hours over and above previously agreed to should always be optional for the nanny. A work agreement should address regular work hours. Moreover, if a family expects you to be available certain hours on an "on call" basis, then these hours should be paid for, regardless if you work them or not. If the parent is expecting you to drop everything during that time to come work if needed, then that is not called "off hours."

Use Vacation Days

You should request to have Paid Time Off (PTO) in your work agreement. Negotiating how much time you get will depend on you, but a minimum amount should be ten days in a calendar year if you work full time. These days can include professional development days and sick days, but, for most nannies, these ten days are in addition to holidays and professional development days.

If you have these in your agreement, use them. Use them to do things that you enjoy or to continue your education. Find out how much notice the family needs before you take time off and have fun.

Building Your Support Community

"You need to find out what refuels and energizes you. If you don't know, experiment, do new things that you never thought you would do, be brave and get outside of your box."
Greta Schraer

You might discover that there is a whole world out there you did not know about. Building your support community is all about finding the things that make you happy and strategically start planning them into your daily, weekly, monthly, and yearly calendar. Don't be afraid to say no to things that don't satisfy you, even if they are things that you have thought for a long time would make you happy. If you are involved in activities outside of work that no longer make you happy, let them go. Find new activities that bring you joy. Set these activities as priorities in your life that only true emergencies will stop you from doing.

If you currently are not doing anything that brings you joy, set goals for yourself and then break them down into attainable pieces so that you can achieve these goals. You will be amazed at how they make you feel.

Time and Energy Suckers

Social media, television shows, movies, video games, and other media can be fun, but they can also suck your time. If you feel like you don't have time to do things that you love, take look at where you are spending your free time. It is easy to go on Facebook to check in with friends and find that hours have passed. This in and of itself is not a bad thing, but if you find that catching up with friends in this way is not bringing you the joy that it should, consider spending time with people in person. Try to set the alarm for your time in the social media world.

TV shows can stir emotions and captivate the imagination, but so can a book. Maybe you miss reading or taking walks, but you find that you spend most nights on the couch in front of the TV. Ask yourself if this is making you happy. Video games, especially the online form, can be another way to interact with people, but they should not be a replacement for spending time with *real* people. Movies can be a wonderful treat, but they can also get expensive. If this is one way that you can interact with friends, then going to the movies may be an excellent choice for after work hours, but ask yourself if you are really enjoying the movies. Maybe there are other activities that not only suck your time but leave you feeling less energetic. It may be time to ditch those activities and find new ones.

It can also be valuable to think about your day and what time you are at your peak. Are you an early riser, waking on your own before you need to be awake? Be strategic and, instead of engaging in activities that waste this time, do something that makes you happy. Are you a night owl? Don't spend your evenings watching a bunch of TV shows; find something else that engages your mind and body and will leave you sleeping soundly and happily.

Self-Care Benefits the Family You Work For

Most employers don't question what their nanny does during hours outside of work. However, if you are trying to convince the parents you work with that you cannot take that extra weekend work, it might be necessary to explain why it is essential for you to engage in activities that bring you joy. Put it in terms that you employer will appreciate. Explain that having a healthy work/life balance will affect the wholeness of her family as well. Tell her that when you have time off, you have more stamina on the job, and you are less likely to get sick and need to take off work. Relate your need for time off to your ability to care for the children and your employer will almost always understand.

Modeling Self-Care for Children

You can start by partnering with the children you care for by bringing attention to

Chapter 13. Self-Care and the Nanny

your body, mind, and emotions at work. Exercise with the children. Shop for healthy food while the children are with you. Cook well-balanced meals together. Be honest about your feelings with the children and they will begin to mirror these healthy habits back to you.

Spend time looking at what wholeness looks like for you. Is faith important to you? Then don't neglect it. Building a community for yourself that will work to build you up rather than tear you down is of the utmost importance. If you don't take care of yourself, you can't take care of others very well and it will show.

GRETA SCHRAER

Greta Schraer has been in the childcare industry for over 20 years. She began working with children at age 12, after becoming a Red Cross-Certified Babysitter and has loved it ever since. In 2010, Greta was the recipient of the International Nanny Association's Nanny of the Year award and she currently serves as the First Vice President of the INA. Starting as a local community for nannies in Cincinnati, Ohio, Greta founded CincyNanny in 2009. Greta has a passion to coach nannies as they progress in their careers, face challenges in their jobs, and seek to excel in the industry. She feels privileged to guide families as they navigate their way through quality care choices for their children. Greta has written for Regarding Nannies, as well

Nanny Basics and Beyond

as articles for the INAVision. Greta is a wife and the mother of two wonderful boys.

CincyNanny.com

Chapter 14. Different Discipline Styles

"Children should learn to make good choices because they want to do the right thing, not just to avoid punishment. This is self-discipline."
Marcia Hall

You probably have tools for guiding children toward appropriate behaviors that you find to be most effective. When you work in the home with other people's children, you usually need to work alongside those parents to raise children who are healthy and well balanced, so that someday they become a productive part of the world. Sometimes the ideas for discipline and guidance that you have will need to be adjusted based on the parents' discipline style. This becomes a concern when you have to work within a discipline style that is not your first choice, one that you are not familiar with, or one with which you disagree.

It is worth noting here that you should never use any form of physical punishment on the children in your care. There are many reasons why this is inappropriate, including the fact that even if the parent has said it is OK, if the children are hurt, the parent could change his mind or deny giving you permission to physically punish his children.

Discipline versus Punishment

Positive Parenting* states that discipline is really about guidance. It is a way to keep children safe as they discover the world. Children need to learn how to manage their feelings, impulses, and actions so they can learn to get along with others. Discipline is also about helping children understand the values that are important to their family.

Many people see punishment as a synonym for discipline, but it is a whole separate act. Punishment is used to control and for retribution. Young children do not commit crimes. Their mistakes call for a corrective disciplinary response. Punishment often interferes with the development of children's internal controls by teaching children that it is someone else's responsibility to control them and decide what behavior is "bad" and what the consequences will be. Children may then conclude that it is OK to misbehave if they can avoid getting caught or if they are willing to accept the consequences.

General Discipline Styles

The first style we will look at is **Uninvolved Parenting**, sometimes referred to as Disengaged or Neglectful Parenting. This parent tends to have trouble meeting children's basic needs and often expects children "to raise themselves." This parenting style is rooted in an emotional or physical issue that the parent has. A parent with this style may have little knowledge about what his children are doing from day to day. He often has few or no rules that the children are expected to follow, and there is very little guidance given to the children.

Typically children who grow up with this type of parenting lack self-worth. They may perform poorly in school and have frequent behavioral problems. They can seem generally unhappy and always on edge because of the lack of any concern for their well-being found under this style of parenting.

Authoritarian Parenting, which is also known as Dictator or "My-way-or-the-highway" Parenting, is where the parent establishes rules and expects children to follow these rules without exception. Children are not usually given reasons for the rules, and there is little or no room for negotiation. Punishments rather than consequences are used, and often these punishments are harmful to the child's development. Sometimes, but not always, these punishments are considered abuse by legal standards.

Children who have grown up with this type of parenting may struggle with self-esteem and have aggressive behaviors. They may lack the ability to problem-solve and make decisions for themselves because they have always been told what to do and when to do it.

Permissive Parenting is sometimes referred to as "kids-will-be-kids" parenting and takes the opposite approach. Parents with this style tend to be lenient and only step in when there's a serious problem, if then. There are few consequences for negative behaviors and the parent often takes on a "friend" rather than a parental role in the lives of the children.

Children who have grown up with this type of parenting may struggle academically and exhibit more behavioral problems. They may also fight with authority and following rules in school. They might have a low self-image.

Authoritative Parenting, also is known as Rules-and-Consequences Parenting, is the type of parenting widely recognized as the most beneficial for children. The parent who uses this style has rules, but there are opportunities for exceptions based on the facts and events. Children are told the reasons behind the rules, and the parent will often consider children's feelings, temperament, and personality when setting limits. Limits might be different based on the needs of the children. Consequences are stressed over punishment, and the use of positive reinforcement is encouraged for appropriate behaviors.

Children who have grown up with this type of parenting tend to be happier and more successful in school and hobbies. They are often good at making a decision and evaluating risks on their own. They tend to become more responsible adults and are generally comfortable expressing their opinions.

Specific Discipline Techniques

Now that we have established the discipline style that is widely recognized as the most effective in helping children to become healthy and well-balanced, let's discuss a number of the most common techniques that a parent might learn and use. This is not an exhaustive list, but understanding these basic techniques can help when speaking with an employer.

Positive Discipline

Positive Discipline* is a program developed by Dr. Jane Nelsen, and is designed to teach young people to become responsible, respectful, and resourceful members of their communities. Positive Discipline teaches essential social and life skills in a manner that is deeply respectful and encouraging for both children and adults (including parents, teachers, childcare providers, youth workers, and others).

Nanny Basics and Beyond

Research tells us that children are hardwired from birth to connect with others and that children who feel a sense of connection to their community, family, and school are less likely to misbehave. To be successful, contributing members of their community, children must learn necessary social and life skills. Positive Discipline is based on the understanding that discipline must be taught and that discipline teaches.

Attachment Parenting

The cornerstone of developmentally appropriate Attachment Parenting* is parental emotional sensitivity to children. Emotional sensitivity refers to a parent anticipating and being sensitive to the children's needs and then attempting to meet those perceived needs. Attachment parenting includes warm, affectionate responses to the children's bids for attention.

Other parenting behaviors that make up the attachment style of parenting include infant-focused prenatal activities; breastfeeding, when possible, to encourage closeness and healthy development; maintaining close physical proximity through frequent touch, carrying, and physical contact and stimulation with the infant; establishing nighttime routines that support an infant's need for closeness; and avoiding long caregiver-child separations. As children age, attachment parenting continues to include age-appropriate proximity maintenance behaviors, age-appropriate levels of touch, a democratic style of communication and problem solving, and the parent's use of inductive reasoning techniques to help children learn positive behaviors. Most of all, regardless of a child's age, attachment parenting refers to a parent's ability to empathize with how a child is feeling and to how a parent views those feelings as valuable and worthy of a parental response.

Conscious Discipline

Conscious Discipline* encompasses four components that empower parents and caregivers to respond consciously instead of unconsciously when reacting to everyday conflict.

Brain State Model: understand how internal emotional states dictate behavior

Seven Powers for Conscious Adults: You cannot teach what you do not know

The Connected Family: Building connections through a culture of compassion

Seven Skills of Discipline: Social-emotional learning

Love and Logic

The Love and Logic* approach is built around the science of crafting caring and respectful relationships. An authentic, loving connection between a parent and his children is the root of a healthy, thriving relationship built on trust and understanding.

Choose Love. Love children so much you are willing to set and enforce limits. This means doing so with compassion.

Choose Logic. Allow children to make decisions, make affordable mistakes, and experience the natural consequences. When balanced with sincere empathy, they develop the following logic: The quality of my life depends on the quality of my choices.

1-2-3 Magic

Effective discipline for children 2 to 12 is an evidence-based, easy-to-learn, and effective parenting program. The 1-2-3 Magic* system can be used with children as young as 18 months through 12 years. Parents and caregivers are in charge, but no arguing, yelling, or spanking is allowed. The system is said to produce results quickly, and its power comes from the fact that it is the only program based on a simple premise: parents (and caregivers) talk too much! Silence speaks louder than words.

Resources for Infant Educators (RIE)

Respect is the basis of the RIE* philosophy. Not only feel respect for babies but demonstrate this respect every time we interact with them. Respecting a child means treating even the youngest infant as a unique human being, not as an object.

Chapter 14. Different Discipline Styles

The goal is an authentic child, a child who feels secure, autonomous, and competent. Cornerstones of this philosophy include
- Trust in the infant's competence
- Sensitive observation
- Care activities that involve the child
- A safe, challenging, and predictable environment
- Time for uninterrupted play and freedom to explore
- Consistency

Nurtured Heart Approach
The Nurtured Heart Approach* is a relationship-focused method founded in The 3 Stands for helping children (and adults) build their Inner Wealth and use their intensity in successful ways. The Nurtured Heart Approach has become a powerful way of awakening the inherent greatness in all children while facilitating parenting, caregiving, and classroom success.

Stand 1: Absolutely No! Refusing to energize negative behavior

Stand 2: Absolutely Yes! Relentlessly energizing the positive

Stand 3: Absolutely Clear! Maintain total clarity about rules that demonstrate fair and consistent boundaries

A parent will not always follow one technique to the letter, but take pieces of those that feel right to him. Often a parent changes his mind about discipline or will at least alter the way that he disciplines based on how a technique has worked for his children in the past. The way a parent disciplines can change a little or a lot over the years, and even changes from one child to the next.

A Parent with Different Techniques than You

Before you accept a job, you should know what the parent's discipline style is. During the interview process, ask questions that lead you to understand his general parenting style and also hone in on the specific techniques he wants to use. You can even ask situation-based questions that will help you see if it is just the parent's desire to respond with the mentioned technique or if he would likely follow through on that technique.

If the parent has made it clear there is a technique to which he holds close, do research on that technique. Maybe it is a technique with which you can become certified. If the parent feels strongly about it, he may even be willing to pay for the classes. Even the act of purchasing a book on your own to better understand the technique can send a powerful message.

Sometimes you will work for a parent who does not fully align with your discipline philosophy. As partners in parenting, you both need to be on the same page when it comes to consequences for the children's negative and positive actions. While it might be hard to work for a parent who does not wholly agree with your discipline, here are several helpful tips.

Know your childcare philosophy, including your preferred discipline style. It is critical for you to know yourself and how you are most comfortable disciplining children. If you are uncomfortable providing harsh punishments, but the parent you work for is expecting you to, you will not enjoy your work.

Understand that while you love the children and have a significant role to play in the situation, the parent is the one who ultimately gets to make the decisions. There are times that the parent might look to you as a guide in the decision-making process, but it is not your place to require parents to choose "your" way.

This might mean that you pass on a job that seems right in every other way or give notice at a position that does not fit you anymore. As long as you behave professionally, there is nothing wrong with it. Not all jobs match every nanny. Finding the right fit is sometimes hard.

Having a deep understanding of the most popular techniques is helpful. This will give you a solid base on what method the parent might choose and will also help you recognize when the parent changes. When the parent seems to shift discipline course or begins merely to let behaviors slide, you have two options.

The first choice is to let it go. Parenting is stressful, and jobs are distracting. Sometimes out of sheer exhaustion a parent will choose to ignore a behavior. If a parent diverges from his normal discipline style now and then, it is probably best to let that go. This does not mean that you alter the way you discipline the children, but that you give the parent the benefit of the doubt that it was an isolated incident.

The second option is to discuss it with him. Sometimes a parent will not realize how far he has slid from the way he intended to parent. A carefully approached conversation can help bring him back on track.

Parents with Non-Ideal Styles

At the beginning of the chapter, I shared details about the four discipline styles that are widely recognized by childcare experts: Uninvolved, Authoritarian, Permissive, and Authoritative. Since the Authoritative style is what childcare experts identify as the ideal parenting style, we need to know how to work with parents who operate in the other three styles. So how, as the nanny, can you work with parents who, either consciously or unconsciously, parent in ways that could be damaging to the children?

By and large, your employer is doing the best that he can with what he is given. Very rarely does any parent really want to hurt children. The parent's default parenting style will be the way he was raised. This is true of everyone. When stress comes, regardless of what he mentally wants to do, he will default to the way he was brought up unless he works very hard to overcome that natural tendency.

Unless the parent has told you otherwise, you should not follow these three styles of parenting. You should not be an uninvolved, permissive, or authoritarian nanny. You should show the children and the parent how authoritative parenting looks. Children have a great ability to adapt to the person they are with, meaning that if the children's parent permits them to do certain things, they can learn that those actions will not be acceptable with you.

How to Work with Uninvolved Parents

Uninvolved parents are parents who have trouble meeting children's basic needs at times. This could be due to illness, addiction, or other extreme stresses of life. You need to be aware if the parent is handing over the responsibilities to you as the nanny because he does not want to be involved, he can't be involved, or he does not know how to be involved. Knowing the reason behind his difficulty attending to his children's needs will help you.

Be clear with the Uninvolved Parent about the parameters and discipline style you will be using with his children. While this parent may relinquish the discipline of the children to you, he needs to be at a minimum comfortable with the discipline choices you'll be making.

Nanny Basics and Beyond

Sometimes a parent who fits this parenting style does so because of a difficulty he is having personally or professionally. It is nice for you to be able to help support the parent by being there with the children, but it is equally important for the parent to be healthy. Remember that you cannot fix him, but you might be able to point him in the right direction. Ultimately, your responsibility is to the children, not the parent. Often children who are raised like this lack self-worth. You will need to work extra hard to build feelings of self-worth in the children. Acknowledge when they work hard, help them to feel good about working toward a goal, and let them do things they are capable of for themselves.

How to work with Permissive Parents

Remember these are parents who tend to be lenient and only step in when there is a severe problem, if then. There are few consequences for negative actions. Be sure to have a conversation with the parent about your authority in the house. It is vital when working with a permissive parent that he recognize and support your authority in the home. If he does not, you will end up with power struggles and children who will quickly run to the parent to "fix" the consequences that you have placed on them.

Permissive Parents might also be going through a trauma that you cannot see. Again, remember that you cannot fix the parent.

Chapter 14. Different Discipline Styles

Frequently, the permissive type parent is laboring under guilt. While you cannot fix this, you can support and encourage him. A Permissive Parent tends to "spoil" his children. Showing children the value of hard work and sacrifice will be especially influential to their self-esteem.

How to work with Authoritarian Parents

Remember these are parents who establish rules and expect children to follow those rules without exception. Harsh punishments are often used. Recognize that often a parent falls into this style because it was how he was raised. Without a firm understanding of the most recent child development studies, the parent will likely believe that the way he was treated is just the way you do it. He is afraid of letting his child misbehave at all because he thinks that any misconduct will lead to his children turning out to be rude and lazy.

These parents will usually want you to follow suit with the way you discipline. While you will need to be comfortable with this role, you can also work to help the child with genuine communication. If the parent insists on punishments for wrongdoing, you can at least explain to the children why they have been given the penalty and how they can learn from it.

Children who have been disciplined with this style can be more aggressive. Having you model calm behavior will help the children to see there is more than one way to act. A parent with this style often controls and fixes everything that goes wrong, and children then have trouble learning problem-solving and decision-making. You will need to provide opportunities for the children to fix problems they have on their own with guidance from you.

Know yourself and what your childcare philosophies and preferred discipline styles are. Ask leading questions in the interview, so things are clear from the beginning. Research the parent's preferred style so you can support him appropriately. Be honest with yourself and the parent about following through on discipline. If you cannot follow through or don't feel supported, you may need to consider your options and remember, not every job is right for you.

* Positive Parenting: positiveparenting.com/discipline-punishment

* Positive Discipline: positivediscipline.com

* Attachment Parenting: attachmentparenting.org.

* Conscious Discipline: consciousdiscipline.com.

* Love and Logic: loveandlogic.com.

* 1-2-3 Magic: 123magic.com.

Chapter 14. Different Discipline Styles

* Resources for Infant Educators: RIE.org.

* The Nurtured Heart Approach: childrenssuccessfoundation.com/about-nurtured-heart-approach.

Nanny Basics and Beyond

Chapter 15. The Parent-Child Bond

"The bond children form with their caregivers as infants provides the first model for what an intimate relationship looks like." Marcia Hall

When you take a job as a nanny, you know that, to do your job well, you need to form a connection with the children in your care. This connection happens at varying speeds and in varying degrees. While this connection is necessary, ultimately the relationship the children have with their parent is the foundation for them. While you may end up being with the children for a long time, their parents will *always* be their parents.

Understanding the importance of this bond and actively working to develop it are two very different things. It may seem unlikely that you can affect a relationship of which you are not a part, but you can have an influence.

What a Bond Does for a Child

Children who feel a secure connection to a primary caregiver are more secure, have a stronger coping mechanism, and are better able to express their feelings.

The bond children form with their caregivers as infants provides the first model for what an intimate relationship looks like. If a bond occurs for children in the first few months of life, it can foster a sense of security and positive self-worth even in infancy. A caregiver's responsiveness to every cry and *coo* can affect the children's social and cognitive development for their entire life. The fact that infants need a strong and continuing bond cannot be understated. It is essential for a healthy life down the road.

The importance of bonding does not end with babies. Children who feel a strong connection to a primary caregiver are more secure, have a better coping mechanism, and are better able to express their feelings.

Anyone who has witnessed what can happen to children who are frequently moved from one home to another can attest to the many issues that the children can face. However, issues like Reactive Attachment Disorder are not only found in the foster care system, where it is typical to find children moving from one home to another. Children who have never felt connected to a parent can also develop symptoms.

Types of Bonds

There are four types of bonds that children can have to a primary caregiver.*

Secure Attachment. When children have found that a primary caregiver is able to meet their needs at least half of the time, this is called "healthy attachment." Healthy attachment is evident in children who are able to cope to a reasonable degree with adversity and are social with other children to the level that their personality allows. These children will also have an age-appropriate amount of self-control.

Avoidant Attachment. Avoidant attachment happens when children have found that their parent is distant or rejecting of their needs most of the time. This type of attachment is evident in a child who avoids healthy relationships with peers and adults.

Ambivalent Attachment. Ambivalent attachment can occur when children have found that their parent is inconsistent with meeting their needs. Sometimes needs are met, and other times they are not, but there is no way to predict at what point their needs will be met, if at all. Ambivalent attachment is evident in children who are frequently anxious.

Disorganized Attachment. Disorganized attachment can manifest itself when children have found that their parent continually and regularly ignores their needs. These children have often had an experience with their parent that leaves them feeling overwhelmed and frightened. Disorganized attachment is evident in children who are unable to regulate their emotions and may be violent.

The relationship children have with their parent lasts far longer than their childhood years and can affect them into adulthood. Whether children need food or an emotional connection, it is crucial that those needs are met by a primary caregiver at least a majority of the time.

Causes of Negative Attachment

Below is a list of possible causes of a negative attachment. It is not an exhaustive list but, as you can see, these events can happen to any child, in any family, and you should know if the children in your care are affected by any of them.

- Physical neglect
- Emotional neglect
- Abuse
- Separation from the primary caregiver
- Changes in primary caregiver
- Frequent moves
- Traumatic experiences
- Parental depression
- Parental addiction to drugs or alcohol

Chapter 15. The Parent-Child Bond

• Un-diagnosed, painful illness, such as colic, ear infections, or others
• Lack of harmony between mother or father and child
• Young or inexperienced mother or father with poor parenting skills.

Stages in Bonding

Bonding in infancy is much more than simply feeding and diapering babies. It involves facial expressions, consistency in sleep patterns, and the ability to understand what the child needs in a reasonable amount of time. Infants will begin to use all five senses to determine the connection, so touch is important. A baby will quickly start to smell and feel, whether it is her primary caregiver meeting her needs or someone else.

Toddlers may be more complicated to bond with, but the need to connect is no less there. Bonding with toddlers involves many of the same experiences as with babies. Now there is an added need for clear boundaries. Toddlers may try to push every limit, but they also have a fundamental requirement for that boundary to be upheld. When the boundary is pushed, and the caregiver does not respond, children feel confused and insecure. Failure to establish and maintain boundaries injures a toddler's connection with the caregiver. Toddlers have the emotional need for the caregiver to keep them safe and, when that does not happen, a connection is not clear.

As children grow and start school, they still require their needs to be met and boundaries to be set. However, their resolution to overcome grows stronger. Children's brains are developing, and new tricks are found to get around the boundaries that are set. Emotions are more sophisticated; the primary caregiver should be reliably consistent in upholding those limits.

Adolescence brings new needs. As children have felt secure within the boundaries of their primary caregiver's walls of protection, they now need to learn to survive outside of those walls. Whether conscientiously understood or not, teens instinctively attempt to escape the boundaries, especially if they are set with too much restriction. Now the primary caregiver needs to alter the way that she is bonding with her teens, in order to both give enough freedom so that the teens can begin to stand on their own two feet, but also so that the teens have the caregiver's support to fall back on.

The Importance of Children's Bond to Parents
It is vital that the children in your care connect with you or any other regular caregiver. In the professional nanny world, it is common for children to form a primary care bond with you. After all, they may spend the majority of their time with you. Unfortunately, I see several problems with this.

Chapter 15. The Parent-Child Bond

No job lasts forever. Very rarely will you stay with children into adulthood and beyond. The trauma children go through when they lose you will be great, but it could be damaging if you are their primary caregiver. It is similar to the trauma that a foster child faces when moved from home to home. It is devastating and life-altering. It's not an event we should want our little ones to have to go through.

You don't make the decisions about their lives. Even if you are the most involved nanny, you do not get to make the most significant decisions of the children's lives. Things like what type of treatment they get if they fall ill or to what school they will go. Depending on your relationship in the home, you may get to make very few decisions. The person who makes those big decisions about their lives should be the one who is most intimately connected to them.

Children want their parents. It is impressive the pull that children have to stay connected to their parent. Even children whose parent has neglected, abused and ignored them for a good part of their life still have an intense desire to be close to a parent. This desire for connection never goes away.

The Nanny's Bond with the Children
The connection you have with the children in your care should not be their primary connection. So, what should your relationship with the children be?

Nanny Basics and Beyond

Of course, your bond should always be a loving and caring one, where you are looking out for their best interests and working to understand what their needs are.

It should be respectful. Respect is a very powerful thing, and when children are shown what it looks like, they will be more likely to give it to others.

It should consist of firm boundaries. As I stated earlier, as children grow, they can only form secure connections with people who provide them with clear boundaries. These boundaries need to be set depending on their needs, personalities, and always in kind and loving ways.

It should be in harmony with that of their parent's bond because you are not attempting to circumvent that. It should be begun in unison with their parent. This is where excellent communication within your relationship with the parent comes into play. You need to understand the children's relationship to their parent so you can work in harmony with that, rather than against it.

Promoting the Bond

So now that we have established the reason children need a primary bond and why their parents should fill that role, let's talk about how you can help to strengthen this bond.

Chapter 15. The Parent-Child Bond

It can be a challenge but here are ten ways you can help encourage the bond in your nanny family.

- Make it clear you understand and respect the relationship the parent has with her children. This can be done in many different ways, but most importantly when talking with her. She may need to be repeatedly reminded that her children want and need that connection as well as the fact that you are not attempting to replace her in that relationship.
- Be understanding when jealousy arises and use this as an opportunity to reinforce that the parent is right.
- Talk about the parent often when she is not home. Children often miss their parent, and it can be more comfortable for the nanny to not mention the parent when she is not around because it can cause sadness. However, children need to talk about a parent when she is not around. This is one way that you can continue to make the parent present even when she is not physically there.
- Find a balance between support to the children and backing up the parents when children confide in you. You may find that children tell you more than they say to their parent. Being the children's confidant can seem helpful, but you

should be encouraging the children to bring the discussion back to the parent. You can support this decision by role-playing how they will discuss a difficult topic with the parent.

- Make a record of your time with the children if the parent feels this is beneficial. The act of helping children make a history of the time they spend with you reinforces the idea that the parent is the primary caregiver and that you are there to support that relationship.
- Reserve "firsts" for parents whenever possible. It can be so hard for a parent to miss those big moments with their children, especially when they are younger. When possible, leave first roll over, crawl, walk, etc., for parents to discover.
- Arrange for a time when the parent can have one-to-one experiences with each child. As a way to support the family, you might suggest that a parent who has more than one child take time to be with each child individually on a regular basis. You can support this by working late occasionally or planning the activity.
- Share with the parent moments when the children missed or positively talked about her. A parent wants to know that she is a part of her children's lives even when she

is not physically present. Make comments like, "George told me today how much fun you two had together this weekend bowling. He really loved that."

- Don't become offended when children seem to prefer their parent over you. The parent should be the most important thing to any child. You are there to support the relationship. I always think of the end of Mary Poppins when the children are off with their parents and Mary is left to leave on her own without a goodbye. It may be bittersweet for you, but this is just how it should be.

- Encourage family rituals to which you are not a part. Maybe you cook the family dinner one night a week, but you leave before the family sits down to eat. Perhaps you prepare the children to take a family bike ride together every night after dinner. You can support that by preparing the children and their bikes to be ready for these activities.

Nurturing the relationship the children have with their parents can be tough. If you work for parents who work long hours or travel a lot, helping to build that bond will be more difficult, but it is not only possible, it is imperative that the link be made and nurtured.

*www.extension.purdue.edu/providerparent/fa
mily-child%20relationships/differenttypesp-
c.htm)

Chapter 16. The Household Manager

"It takes a lot to balance to meet all the needs of the children and the responsibilities of the household."
Karen Yatsko

I spoke with Karen Yatsko about her experience as a nanny and household manager. Karen has worked for many families as a household manager and had a lot of wisdom to share on the matter.

Your responsibilities within the household will vary greatly. Often when children are younger, those obligations focus directly on the children and the spaces in the home that the children use. Children's laundry, children's dishes, and play areas will almost always be your duty. As children get older, and start taking on more responsibility and begin attending school during the day, you may want to stay with the family. If so, you will want to transition into being a household manager as well as a nanny.

What is it?

A household manager is someone who is hired by the owners of a home to take care of a variety of tasks that are needed to maintain the owners' property. When you as a nanny take on the responsibility of household manager, it means that you are tasked with a specific list of duties in addition to those relating to the children. These duties could include additional laundry, dishes, and other cleaning, as well as cooking for the whole family. It usually involves shopping for food and other supplies the family might need, plus other errands the parents require, like picking up dry cleaning. It often means that you manage the calendar for the whole family and make travel arrangements for family trips. In larger households, you may work with the other household staff, who deep clean the home, do landscaping, maintenance around the house, and maintain a security system. You could be asked to manage parties and other events. The family may even have you coordinate renovation projects around the property. Sometimes you may manage more than one home. Exactly what your responsibilities are would be up to you and your employer. These responsibilities should be laid out in the work agreement.

In what Kind of Homes will I Work?

Many people assume that as a nanny who is employed as a household manager, you will be working in a large home with many staff members. This can be true. Sometimes it is the responsibility of the household manager to supervise other staff, from maids to the lawn service. It is also likely that you would be employed by an average family where parents work long hours and need the extra help around the house.

No two families are the same, so it is important to understand what the scope of your household manager duties will be and the condition of homes you manage.

Is it Right for You?

Becoming a household manager can be a great way to extend a position with a family you love when the children go to school. The situation can be a win-win for you and the parents, but it must be thoughtfully considered and executed to work well.

To be effective in a position where household managing is also part of the job, you need to be able to adapt to many different situations and be able to take on tasks that you might not ever have done before. For instance, if a parent says, "Can you get someone fix the toilet?," you need to be able to figure out how to hire someone reputable to do that, supervise the work, and then pay the bill. If you have never done that before, you need to be able to learn on the job and continue to work until the job is done, and done well.

You should also be resourceful, meaning that you can come up with wise and efficient solutions to the problems that are in the home. For instance, there may be projects within the house that your employers do not even realize need to be done. An effective household manager will find these projects, research solutions including costs comparisons of vendors, and present the suggested solution to the employer for approval before implementing and supervising the fix.

You should have strong social and directing skills. Part of this job is working with other staff in the home and outside contractors, like a cleaning service or landscaper. You will need to be able to discuss the needs of the employers in a way that is pleasant, but you are also able to hold people professionally accountable if the job does not meet expectations.

You should possess the ability to work independently without the need to be continuously supervised. Being someone who can set goals autonomously will help you to achieve excellence in this type of position. There will be many times where your employers will merely give you a task and expect you to keep following through until its completion. They will not check in with you frequently to make sure that you are doing it, but they will expect it to be done on time. If you are unable to complete tasks without reminders, this might not be the right job for you.

You should be a detail-oriented person so that the jobs you are asked to do are done with consideration of all the smaller aspects that are so important to a good outcome. Multi-tasking will be imperative to you in this job because you will have many projects being worked on at the same time. If you get easily confused about details or can do only one thing at a time, this might not be the job for you.

You will need to be highly organized, with the ability to get proper systems and processes in place quickly. There will be moments when projects need to be completed quickly, or a plan will need to change at the drop of a hat. You will need to be able to make decisions about that project fast, and if you have appropriate systems in place and can work under pressure, you will be fine.

"A great household manager is prepared for anything and keeps track of everything." Karen Yatsko

A household manager will need to be a team player and have strong communication skills. The family is a team, and you are part of the team. Everyone in a team has a job, and you should know your role. When you are unclear about your job, you will need to be able to ask quick and descriptive questions so that you can fully understand what is expected of you.

Having many skills in many areas is helpful for this job, especially skills with technology. Technology dictates more and more of our lives. Keeping up with the latest technologies will not only help you understand what is expected of you but will help you to find solutions. Strong accounting skills are also valuable because there are many times that you will be entrusted with the employer's money. For your protection, you will need to be able to keep track of and record expenses.

You need to be able to set boundaries for yourself. It is tempting to answer phone calls, text messages, and emails during your off hours. Your employer will come to rely on you for all his household needs. You need to decide for yourself what your boundaries will be and then communicate them to your employer.

Above all else, you need to have respect for the privacy of your employer. You may be asked to sign a nondisclosure agreement, but even if you are not, you should act as if you have. What you do for the family, and everything else about the home, should not be shared with anyone. If you do sign a nondisclosure agreement, make sure you have a full understanding of its scope, so that you do not unknowingly break it.

Chapter 16. The Household Manager

Melding the Two Jobs

"The transition from nanny to include household manager can be beneficial to all, but it can also be a challenge to change the nature of a job. It will be new for everyone. Talking with someone who has made this transition can be helpful." Karen Yatsko

Being a nanny/household manager is not easy. It takes a lot of practice and patience to balance the needs of the children and the responsibilities of the household. It is crucial that you be realistic about the time you have to accomplish all the tasks. There is only so much time in the day, and, as the person caring for the children, it should be stated clearly and up front that your primary responsibility is to the children. Make it clear that the children's needs come first.

There are days when children take extra time. Maybe something happened at school, and you need to make special time to talk to the children, or they bring home extra homework, and that needs your attention. Children come home sick from school or have an unexpected day off. It is a great benefit for the parent to have you already home ready to care for the children, but that may leave other tasks undone because the children needed you.

Nanny Basics and Beyond

It is important to review your position periodically, paying close attention to the tasks related to household management. You will want to make sure that the parent is happy with your work. Be honest about the feedback you give on assigned tasks. Just because you are a household manager, that does not mean that you are willing to take on every little job for the parent. There is a difference between a personal assistant and a household manager. Be sure that you draw the line and make the boundaries clear.

If you are interviewing for a position where the family already has children in school, the parent may have a good idea of what specific responsibilities he wants you to take on. Be sure to get a clear understanding of this and how much time he expects you to devote to "household management" before you accept the position.

Attend industry conferences and events. Many events have workshops focused on the household management side of things, especially DEMA (Domestic Estate Management Association). DEMA* has local chapters in the US with monthly programs that can help you if you have more home responsibilities. It may even have supporting vendors in your area, which will help you handle this oftentimes challenging job.

Chapter 16. The Household Manager

"It's important to keep learning. As a household manager, being a "jack of all trades" can pay off. Knowing a bit about a lot of things can help you find the best solutions for your employer's home."
Karen Yatsko

KAREN YATSKO

Karen Yatsko has been a professional nanny for more than 29 years, many of those as a household manager. Karen is a longtime member of the International Nanny Association, serving on its Board of Directors for six years, and behind the scenes in many capacities. She has been a speaker at several conferences, served on a conference committee, and joined several discussion panels. Karen was nominated for the INA Nanny of the Year Award in 1994, has received her 25-year INA Service Pin Award, passed the INA Credential Exam, and currently serves on the Education Committee. In 2018, Karen was given the INA Meritorious Service Award.

Karen was nominated for the Child Caregiver of the Year award by *Parents Magazine* in 1998. She was a co-presenter at the 1998 NAEYC Conference in Toronto, Canada, speaking on "Today's Career Nanny." Karen is also a member of the Domestic Estate Managers Association and is also a supporter and attendee of Nannypalooza and National Nanny Training Day.

Karen has specialized in Household Management for many years and has now completed her courses as a Newborn Care Specialist.

NewbornCareByKaren.com

* DomesticManagers.com

Nadia 9

SECTION III:
SPECIALIZED
SITUATIONS

Nanny Basics and Beyond

Chapter 17. Families during Trauma

"While helping the family through stress and trauma, remember that it is first your responsibility to care for the children and their needs." Marcia Hall

No nanny wants it to happen, but whether it is obvious a family is going through a traumatic event when you take the job or crisis occurs once you are already in a position, you will find yourself working for a family during a time of trial. A child you are caring for develops a serious illness, developmental delay, or is diagnosed with behavior or emotional issues. A parent you work for could be struggling with addiction, illness, infidelity, or marital friction. Parents could be in the middle of a separation, divorce, or start dating again after divorce. The family could be moving or have had a death in the family. Strained financial or employment situations can cause drama in the family as well as abuse.

In many of these situations, especially those directly dealing with the children, your role is more obvious. In other situations, it may be difficult to find your place. It is best to ask the parent what role she would like you to have if you are unsure. Your goal is to be helpful to the family. Here are a number of actions you can take to help relieve the stress felt by a parent and provide support to the children as they go through the stressful time.

Watch For Signs

Signs that the family might be struggling are not always visible. You will want to watch for hints. Parents might be more irritable when they come home from work. You might see symptoms of depression. A parent who is suddenly unavailable to her children or suddenly obsessed with them. A parent who is normally kind and respectful might become harsh and yell at you and the children. Your employer might begin confiding in you in ways that she has not before. These are all hints that something is happening in her life, and it can be a signal to you to offer additional support to her.

Empathy and Hope

No person is perfect. If the trauma in the family is a direct result of a parent's actions, it is important to remember that we all make

Chapter 17. Families during Trauma

mistakes. Finding fault with one or both parents will not be helpful, and it can make a tense situation even worse. Respond to the parent who has made mistakes from a place of compassion. Have hope that the parent can move forward from this situation and be better. Do not focus on the past, but look to the future and the better choices your employer will make.

Be Neutral

It is imperative that you avoid taking sides in the situation involving two parents. You need to remain neutral and fair-minded. Even if you agree with one parent, you need to remember that you are a role model for the children, who love both parents. The children should not be asked to take sides either. If they are being coerced into picking one parent's side, it is your job to protect them and insist that they are not put in the middle.

If an obvious error causes the trauma on the part of either parent, you need to be polite and positive to the offending parent at all times. The children will be looking to you for clues on how to respond. If they sense that you disapprove of the actions of their parent, they will either become angry at you as a way of defending their parent or they will become angry at the parent. Neither of these outcomes is desirable, so remain respectful towards each parent.

You need to discuss the situation with both parents, especially in cases that divide them. Doing so will not only help you better define your role through the event but discussion will help keep you on neutral ground as you navigate your time with the family. It is best to do this in a face-to-face meeting with both parents. It is easy for you to be put in the middle, but if you are in the habit of sitting down regularly with both parents, this will be less likely to happen. If it is not possible to sit down with both parents at the same time, then give the same message to each parent. The core of your message should be identical. Avoid personal emails and text messages that are negative between you and one parent. This will tend to pull you into one side or the other.

United Message

It cannot be stressed enough how important it is for you and the parents to send a unified message to the children during a time of trauma. You need to understand what message your employers want you to pass along to the children. When there is a death in the family, that means you should understand what is being communicated regarding death and an afterlife. You should support the parents' viewpoint on this because sending mixed signals on any traumatic event will not help the children. Even if one parent states that you can share your personal opinion with the children, the parent should know what that is so when the children talk to their parents there are no surprises.

Learn For Yourself

If the event happening in the family is something you are already knowledgeable about, sharing your insight with the parent can be a way for you to support her. Along with sharing your knowledge, you should also share books, articles, websites, or resources that provide quality, trusted information.

If the family is going through something you are unfamiliar with, educate yourself about it. You can do your research by reading books or taking classes on the topic. If one of the children gets diagnosed with ADHD and you don't know much about it, pick up books from the library or look for a workshop you can take on the subject. Many times doctors or hospitals have helpful resources for adults when parents or children receive a diagnosis.

When children are diagnosed with physical, mental, or emotional issues, the most stressful part for the parent is often not knowing anything about the topic. Working alongside the parent as she learns about her child's diagnosis can be a way to strengthen the team and help everyone get through the difficult time. Your active interest will also show the parent exactly how valuable you are in her children's lives and how you are supporting the family as a unit.

Change in Hours

Take a look at your work hours when a crisis occurs. In many traumatic family situations, adding extra hours would help immensely. It can be helpful for the parent to know that you are willing to work overtime and be with the children while she deals with whatever it is she needs to deal with. For instance, if the parents are going through marital counseling, it might be helpful for you to offer to work additional evenings so that they can attend their sessions together. If parents are separated and suddenly the children are going between two houses, it can be an enormous support to both parents and children for you to help transition everyone by being present to transport and settle the children into the new home.

Activity Adjustment

Planning activities outside the home can help divert the children's attention and relieve the stress that they feel in the situation. Plan fun activities in which they don't often get to participate.

If the family is in the middle of a move, taking the children to the new neighborhood to see the playgrounds and other fun places in the area can not only be a way to divert their attention but it can help the children ease the stress that they feel in the move.

Chapter 17. Families during Trauma

Additional Responsibility

If the situation occupies the parent, specific responsibilities she has in the home might not get done. You could offer to do extra planning and organizing. For instance, you might need to take the children to routine doctor appointments or extracurricular activities that are generally not your responsibility. If you are willing to take on additional household responsibilities, it would relieve weight on your employers to know that specific household duties will not be neglected while they are spending time dealing with the situation. Perhaps this means that you arrange to have repairs in the home done or take on more of a household manager position for a time.

Boundaries

When taking on any additional hours or responsibilities, it is best to accurately state in writing what you are willing to do and for how long. You want to be supportive, but crisis situations can last a while, and both you and the parent need to have a realistic understanding of what you are willing to do so that you don't feel you are being taken advantage of if the situation continues longer than expected. Decide on a timeframe that you are agreeing to these extra responsibilities, and decide when you will follow up with your employer when that time is up.

Additional responsibilities might mean that you want to ask for a raise at some point in the future, but, more than that, everyone needs to understand how the job has changed with the added stress in the family.

Look Long-term

Sometimes the job changes so much that it is almost unrecognizable from the position that you agreed to take. When there is a lot of ongoing chaos in the family, you should always ask yourself if this is still the right job for you. Though you love the children and have compassion for the parent, it may be hard to be honest with yourself. While it is a benefit for children to have stability in any of these traumatic situations, you also need to care for yourself. If the job no longer fits you or what you feel you are capable of doing, you are ultimately responsible for yourself above anyone else.

If you know you want to stay with the family but the extra stress is too much for you to take on alone, you could discuss cutting back your hours and finding someone else to take some of those hours. You can consider an extended vacation to recoup, so you can come back to the job refreshed and ready to help to a higher degree.

In fact, the stress of being a support to the whole family might be so great you feel you need a counselor to help you. Discuss this with the parent and ask her to consider paying for this so

Chapter 17. Families during Trauma

that you can continue to help the family. It is
not easy to be around a family in crisis, and
there is no shame in the helper getting help. It is
better to seek out the guidance you need before
you burn out and end up quitting. Be open and
honest about this need with the family from the
start, and you will be able to help support them
in the long-term.

Help Children Process

As a nanny, issues with development—both
emotional and physical—fall within your role.
The way you support the children will be directly
related to the crisis they are facing.

If a child has a long-term illness or has
been diagnosed with an exceptional need, being
a loyal support to the child adds stability. The
child needs that stability while wrestling with
how to maintain a healthy body and mind. One
of the most important roles you have is to help
the child process emotion.

The death of a person in the immediate
family, like a parent or sibling, will likely be the
most difficult situation children will ever face.
Often children don't know how to process their
feelings because they don't know if what they
are feeling is normal. Books and articles for
older children can help them work through their
emotions.

You and the parents can help guard the
children against some specifics of the stress in
the home, but no matter how hard you try, the

children will always feel the stress. Unless they are very young, it is best to be honest with them about the truth. You and the parent should be willing to have a conversation about what is happening. This is one reason why it is so important for parents and the nanny to be on the same page about the events, so when the children do ask questions, you are both sending the same message and the children do not get more confused.

When the children ask questions, be ready to not only answer the questions but support the emotions behind the questions. For instance, if children ask, "Why is mommy always at the doctor?," be ready to share a basic reason. It should be the truth, but not give details that aren't age appropriate. Beyond that, you can follow the children's question with one of your own. You can say, "Your mommy has been at the doctor a lot lately. Do you miss her when she is not here? What activities do you like to do with her the most? How does it make you feel when she comes home? If you could say something to her right now, what would you say?" You can even suggest that the children make something for mom when they miss her.

Watch for signs that the children might be feeling worried or frustrated but are not able to articulate their feelings. Many times when children of all ages are afraid, this concern comes out in the unexpected ways. Children who are worried often misbehave or change their attitude. Worried children often resort to anger or sadness at things that are not important. For instance, children who have a parent who is stressed at work might start lashing out at siblings when their parent is due to come home, especially if the parent has been irritable when he first comes back. When children start acting out or change behaviors suddenly, it is essential for you to help them find the words to the emotions they are feeling.

Play acting can be a great way to allow the emotions the children are unable to understand or communicate to come out. Dolls, stuffed animals, an action figure, or really anything can provide a window into the real feelings children have. Pay close attention to what the children say and do as they are playing.

While you don't want to project your feelings onto the children, it is helpful not to hide all your emotions from them. Children often feel that their strong emotions are inappropriate, especially if they have been shamed or told they could not show their feelings in the past. When you express your feelings in a positive manner, it can teach children how they should show their emotions.

If you sense that the children are feeling frustrated or hurt by the stress occurring in the household, you can share similar feelings about an unrelated topic. This will help the children see that the feeling is OK, but that there are healthy ways to express it. This can also be done through make-believe and play. Children are more likely to open up during play.

Ultimately, your role in the children's lives is to be the person they can go to. Validate the feelings they can express and help them figure out what emotions they might not be able to communicate with non-assuming questions like, "I notice that you threw that bowl when your dad told you he would not be home. Is there a reason you did not like what he said?"

Once you help the children pinpoint their emotions, you can help them think of a solution to the problem. Maybe the child threw the bowl because his dad has been working late hours lately and has not been able to read his bedtime story recently. Perhaps you can help the child put words to this and talk to the dad, asking for one night a week to still have story time. If the child comes up with a solution, it is best that the child execute the solution, with your help. This means that you avoid going to the parent with the solution, but that you help the child find the right words. When possible, you should be the "helper" in this situation, rather than the person who "fixes" the problem.

Sometimes it is not possible to solve the problem because what the children need is someone to listen and empathize. It is crucial that you not try to solve the children's problem with giving into unhealthy behaviors or rewarding them with stuff. This will not help the children work through the trauma and will

Chapter 17. Families during Trauma

reinforce unhealthy behaviors. It is also unwise in most situations to distract children who are feeling hurt or angry for long periods of time. Instead, help the children find a positive outlet for the strong and genuine emotions they are feeling.

Protect Children

Protecting the children means that you stand guard as to what they see and hear. You cannot always protect them, but sometimes you can help by removing them from the location as often as possible.

It is critical to remember that unless you have a degree in psychology, you are not a therapist, and it might be important that the child see a professional psychologist to get the right help. Advocating for this to the parent is one huge way that you can help protect the children.

Protecting a child also means that if you suspect abuse or neglect in the home of the children or of a parent, you take action. Domestic violence knows no socio-economic class and can happen to any child. As a paid caregiver, in most places you are a mandated reporter, so if you suspect child abuse, you are legally obligated to report it. For your protection and to correctly report it, you should document the children's injuries in a form that cannot be altered. Photo documentation in many situations is necessary. An email to the parents

269

documenting any injuries you find immediately is also essential. This documentation may protect you from blame and might expose a pattern of injury that you otherwise would not notice.

As a professional nanny, you should always know the process of reporting abuse wherever you are located. In the US, you can look up the Child Protective Services Department of your local government with a simple internet search. The process is similar in most states, but research the process so that you should know what to expect. For most locations, you call a phone number and say that you are reporting suspected abuse of children in your care. You will be asked questions. While many places allow you to give a report anonymously, other areas require a name. Often, giving an anonymous statement is not regarded as significant as when the caller gives his or her name. Unfortunately, not all Child Protective Services departments will withhold the caller's name, either, so there is a possibility that the parent you work for might find out that it was you who reported it. You might also become part of the investigation, which is why the documentation is so critical.

Reporting neglect or abuse is never emotionally or professionally easy to do, but is the right thing to do. Should you need guidance, the U.S. Department of Health and Family

Chapter 17. Families during Trauma

Services* has a handbook for childcare workers that might be helpful to you.

Spousal abuse is also serious and can be hard to identify. You may hear stories from the children in your care or you might see the evidence of it yourself. The National Coalition Against Domestic Violence* says that children who live in homes where there is domestic violence also suffer abuse or neglect at high rates.

You may or may not be able to change the situation. First and foremost, if you feel unsafe, you should leave. Either way, you can still protect the parent and the children by reporting your suspicions. There is a National Domestic Violence Hotline* that can help.

Tips for Talking About Touchy Subjects

Many nannies find it challenging to have honest discussions with the parent they work for about trauma in the home. Having these candid conversations is imperative but should be done with great care. Use your judgment and observations about when is a good time to talk or meet. Avoid having these discussions when the children are around. Highlight your experience or research on the topic and focus on the fact that you take your job as nanny and protector of the children seriously. Their health, safety, and well-being is your top priority.

While many topics are within your purview to discuss with parents, suspicions of mistreatment and abuse are in a level all their own. If you suspect that a child is being mistreated or abused by a teacher, coach or other non-family member or close family member, it might be a conversation you want to have with the parents. Be sure to avoid using the word "abuse" and discuss things as "events" or "episodes."

However, if you suspect that a parent, family member, or close friend of the family is abusing the children, this is not something you should discuss with the parents. You need to document any concerns and report this to the authorities.

Parental addiction is also a topic that you should not bring up to an employer. Do what you can to protect the children in this instance but you cannot control what the parent is doing. If you feel that the addiction is causing abuse or neglect, document your specific concerns and report them to the authorities.

When discussing trauma within your purview with the parent, you will want to remember the following.

Perspective: Do you see this from only your perspective? What is the view that the parent and children have? Look at the situation from all angles.

Investigate: Read up on the topic so that you can speak about it from a scientific- or research-based viewpoint and not just from your own experience.

Chapter 17. Families during Trauma

Prepare to Walk Away: Realize that dealing with the situation might mean that this job ends.

Who first: Will you be talking with both parents or one parent?

Write out your thoughts: It is always beneficial to at least write out an outline of what you want to say. You should have

- A positive about the parent or situation
- An observation about the situation
- A concern that you see
- Several possible solutions to the problem
- Then conclude with another positive remark about the parents or situation

First contact: This might be a short message stating that you would like to talk but should also include a statement that you would like to discuss it soon. Give several times that you are willing to speak with the parents or parent outside of working hours.

Discussion: It will be hard and it might be uncomfortable, but no situation is ever resolved unless a conversation is had. Remember to be willing to help with a solution.

Take care of yourself: Remember to ask yourself if this is the right place for you and to seek the support you need to stay healthy.

Real-Life Examples

There are thousands of examples of trauma you might face with the children for which you care. I cannot review every scenario. However, the following few examples might help you.

Example A:

Mom and dad are always fighting. You have noticed it bothering the child. What do you do?

- No judgment: Make sure that you don't project your negativity onto your charge.
- Extra patience: Realize that some of the behaviors the child is exhibiting are her way of lashing out.
- Help the child express and validate her feelings: Encourage dialogue about the topic.
- Ask open-ended, non-leading questions: "How does that make you feel?," "What would you like to say to them?"
- Remind the child that everyone argues: You could provide an example of when you got into an argument with someone who you are still very close to, or you could share an example of a TV show or book that the child likes where the characters argued.
- Suggest an outlet: Does the child like to color? Put together a box of supplies that the child can go to when the parents fight. Does the child enjoy basketball? Make a plan to play ball when the arguments happen.
- Use imaginary play to let the child express emotions: This can be appropriate for a

young child who doesn't have the language or emotional intelligence to communicate well.

- Encourage conversation but don't suggest it: It is not the child's responsibility to go to the parents to try to fix things. However, if the child wants to speak to the parents about it, plan how, when, and with what words the child will do it.

Example B:

The three-year-old boy in your care seems to have a speech delay. The parent says that boys take longer to talk. What do you do?

- Research. Read everything you can about speech delays so that when the parent is ready, you have a base of professionally backed knowledge.
- Work on verbal skills at home. While you are not a speech therapist, you can find ways to help with language and focus on this area when you care for the child.
- Highlight the good and the concerning moments. Make sure to highlight moments when the child struggled to communicate but don't make everything negative. Be sure to share about the positive moments of growth too.
- Work with the parents. When the parent is ready to discuss it, make sure that you express that you want to work as a team to help the child overcome this obstacle.

- Their idea. Sometimes the best way to get a parent on board with the need for extra help is to plant the idea in their head and let it grow. Don't be quick to say that it was your idea, but instead let the parents come to their conclusions and then agree with them.
- Remain positive. The child can and will overcome this obstacle, and having a team of adults who love the child will help.

Nannies by nature are nurturers, which means that you want to be able to take care of everyone. While helping the family through stress and trauma, remember that it is first your responsibility to care for the children and their needs. It can be easy to be sucked in to trying to solve every problem for the family. Know your limits and don't be afraid to stick by them.

* U.S. Department of Health and Family Services:
childwelfare.gov/pubs/usermanuals/childcare

* National Coalition Against Domestic Violence: ncadv.org

* National Domestic Violence Hotline: thehotline.org/help/help-for-friends-and-family

Chapter 18. Separated Families

"You are often able to step back and see a different perspective. You can be valuable to the parents as well as the children." Kellie Geres

To better understand this type of job, I spoke with Kellie Geres who has worked with divorced and separated families for 20 of her 30 years in the industry.

With nearly half of all marriages ending in divorce and still other families having parents who are not married, chances are good that you will work with a family that "co-parents" during your career. You may interview with families who are divorced or separated or the parents you have worked with for years might one day drop the bombshell that they are separating.

Either way, you will want to know how to navigate this challenging job.

Personal Characteristics that are Helpful

A job working with separated or divorced parents is not right for everyone. Often these jobs are high stress, and they can be chaotic. Most of the time, you need to be able to take direction from multiple parents that may or may not be contradictory. You need to avoid being put in the middle of disagreements that come up. It also requires that you know what your hot buttons are so that you can set firm boundaries based on them. Ultimately, you will need to understand how the parents want you to fit into the family, and you will need to make sure that you are comfortable being in that place.

> "Working for parents who are divorced or separated will take a person with the ability to manage a strong emotional attachment with the children."
> Kellie Geres

This means that you are willing and able to stick with the family to provide the support needed. You should not feel guilty if you decide that you cannot work for a family that is separated, but, if you do stay, you need to understand that you are providing much-needed stability for the children.

Chapter 18. Separated Families

Finding a New Normal

Like the loss of anything, parents and children will go through many emotions when separation occurs. These emotions can take the form of the five stages of grief: denial, anger, bargaining, depression, and acceptance. You might even find that you pass through these stages. As the child in your care learns about the separation and begins to move through the steps, it is important to remember that everyone is trying to find a new normal, and that it takes time to adjust. It is essential to keep an open dialogue with both parents and discuss all the issues that come up, particularly with regard to how the process is affecting the children.

What will the new situation mean? Will children be at both homes? A family may move the children from one house to the other, and another family may leave the children in one home and have the parents come and go depending on who has custody. Are there any unique situations like this happening? How does this affect your job and pay? Who do you "report" to now? Are there restrictions on your communication with family members?

You should not only discuss these questions but you need to get the answers in writing. This is the type of change that should prompt you to update your work agreement, because the nature of the job is changing. If you are starting a new position where the parents are already separated or divorced, be sure to add these details to the work agreement from the beginning of your employment. It is important to have these conversations up front because the better prepared everyone is, the smoother the transition will be.

Communication

It is necessary to find new and effective ways to communicate among all adults. Find a method where documentation can be shared with everyone, so that if an issue arises, there is one place where all parties can go in order to find out what was intended. You may need to give regular reminders to the parents to use this tool. Parents are busy, and, just like you and the children, they are trying to find their new normal. An excellent way to remind the parents is by encouraging the parents at the moment when you have seen the tool used effectively, saying something like, "Thank you for adding that new appointment to the calendar. I was afraid we would forget. I am glad we have this tool to remind each other." Many times separated parents don't see the benefits of using these tools, so you need to shine a spotlight on those positive outcomes.

There are a host of topics to discuss with co-parents when setting up a communication system. Keeping track of homework and notes from the teacher, scheduling out-of-school activities, vacations, and holidays, as well as assigning the chores the children are expected to do at each home are all important to the cohesion of family life. Managing school report cards and parent-teacher conferences are crucial. The list is endless, which is why it is essential to find a system that works for everyone.

At times you will work for only one of the co-parents. You will need to understand what kind of communication your employer wants you to have with the other parent. Make sure that you clearly understand what type of information you are allowed to relay between the parents. You should always be pleasant to the other parent, but there might be times when you need to be strong and say, "No." Remember that you are there to protect the children, not make life easier for the other parent. Don't take the reaction of this parent personally and discuss any interaction you have with the parent who employs you.

Organization

While you may be tasked with management and orderly running of the home the children live in, when the children live in two homes or go back and forth between separated parents, you may be responsible for not only the organization of one house but two distinct dwellings and maybe more. This means that you will need to make sure that there are appropriate supplies, toys, and clothes at both homes, in addition to making sure that anything that is needed at both houses makes it to its required destination. You will have to organize school supplies, homework, sports gear, uniforms, musical instruments, and a myriad of other items. You will need to help organize where the older children's school projects are being completed. How will all the supplies get from one home to the other? You will have to plan not only where the children will be that evening but plan for later in the week and even the week after that.

The key to making this all work is to keep the priorities at each house consistent. As much as possible, both parents need to understand and comply with the children's routines and schedules. There will be certain things that will change, but holding tight to a few core traditions that take place in both homes can help the children adjust to this new normal.

Changes in Children

When a parental separation first happens or there are changes to the arrangement, you can be confident that it will affect the children. Even when co-parents have the best possible relationship and the transitions are smooth, children will feel the stress of the adjustments. You and the parents will need to prepare for unexpected behaviors from the children and employ an extra level of patience. All adults need to provide a united front when it comes to rewards and consequences.

Chapter 18. Separated Families

When children go through a major stress, like divorce, some will act out, trying to take control of a part of their lives. However, you need to be watchful of not only children who act out: sometimes it is the children who seem to glide through the transition who are in the most danger down the road. These seemingly easy-going children are often bottling up their emotions. At some point, there will be a release. It might be months or even years later, but the situation is affecting them. It is common when there are multiple children in a household for at least one of them to seem fine with the situation, but be struggling inside. So don't ignore the quiet child; sometimes that is the child who needs the most help. Help all the children in your care to find a healthy way to express their emotions about the situation.

Divorce is never easy. The whole family may, in the long run, be better off living in two separate homes, but when it first happens, the children will want to keep everything the same, even if that means their parents stay together and fight. It is a process that children need to move through, and it may take more help than you can offer. There should be no stigma attached to children or adults seeking professional mental health counseling. It is far better for children to visit a therapist while they are young and can work to find tools to handle their complex emotions than it is for them to grow up without adequate help and find themselves with trust and bonding issues as adults. As the nanny, supporting the need for a child to see a professional therapist might be the most valuable thing you can do.

There will be times that you need to be the voice for the children who cannot stand up and express what they need. Don't be afraid to kindly but firmly advocate for the things that you know the children need. Often, when parents are first going through a separation, it is hard for them to see the events clearly.

The Dos and Don'ts

While it might be tempting, there are a number of things that it is vital you *don't* do when you work for parents who are either starting this transition or are already separated or divorced.

Don't approach parents about their marital relationship. If you suspect there are issues in the relationship, you should keep this to yourself. The only time you should approach the parents about divorce or separation is if the children have mentioned something to you about the topic. Repeat what the children have said and ask how you should handle that topic in the future.

Do ask what your role should be. When the parents inform you of an impending divorce or separation, you will want to ask them what role they want you to play in the process. What will they communicate with the children? What would they like you to say to the children? Take your cues on how to act and what to say from the parents. Make sure you clear any supportive comments and stories that you wish to tell the children with the parents.

Don't pick sides. There might be situations where you agree with one parent more than the other, but don't say this to either parent and don't project this to the children. It is so important that you remain neutral, for yourself and for the children.

Do strive to understand why both parents are acting the way they are. Even if you disagree with their actions, you need to respect them.

Don't get too close. It is equally important that you not become too close with one parent, especially if you work for both parents. This can cause many problems down the road and will quickly lead to you picking sides.

Do speak in a friendly way with both parents. If one of them tries to push you to pick sides, just state that, for the sake of the children, you feel it is best that you remain neutral about the specifics of the separation. Encourage that parent to talk with a friend or family member or see a counselor, but don't try to become a sounding board for venting.

Don't become the messenger between parents, and don't allow the children to be either. Co-parents need to find their own way of communicating with each other. Children are often quick to step in and try to mediate their parents' relationship. As the nanny, you need to be firm that it is not the children's job to be the communicator in the relationship. Be firm with parents and children.

Do set up a dependable system of communication. As the nanny, it is your responsibility to help set up the communication system, but it is not your job to actively relay information long term. That is the point of the system: both parents can personally talk to one other.

Don't avoid the tough issues with your employers. You might think that, eventually, the parents will get better at communication or that specific responsibilities thrust on you are there just for the time being. However, without clearly defining a timeline or list of new responsibilities, you will end up doing that extra work indefinitely, without compensation for it. The situation will not get better on its own. It is going to take action to build a positive co-parenting relationship.

Do speak up. If you notice that you or the children are being put in the middle of disagreements, assert yourself and speak up. If you see that the children are missing time with one of the parents, suggest that parent find time to be with the children. Go out of your way to make sure that the quiet, go-with-the-flow child has a voice that is heard.

Don't ever share information that you don't have permission to share about the family on social media or with personal friends. Doing this is unprofessional in and of itself, but many people thrive on gossip. Families going through a separation deserve time to heal and transition. It is not your story to tell.

Do share required information with the people who need it. You might need to communicate essential facts with teachers, principals, counselors, or friends whom the children visit frequently, but you should only share information that the parents have permitted you to share.

Don't try to do this on your own. While it is not your story to tell, it might be necessary for you to seek confidential and professional help from those who have worked with separated and divorced families before. This can be in the form of a counselor or a network of professional caregivers who can help you. Kellie started a support group for nannies in this situation. You can contact her for more information.

Do take time off if you need it. As the nanny for children whose parents are going through a separation or are divorced, you know that you are a stabilizing factor in their lives. You still need to find time to rejuvenate yourself. Take the time you need so you can give the entire family your very best.

"Having a position with a separated or divorced family can be a good job—but

may not be for everyone. Know who you are and what you are capable of."
Kellie Geres

With your help, a tumultuous separation between parents does not need to throw the children's lives into total chaos. You can make a big difference to children in this situation, and it might be the most critical role you take on.

KELLIE GERES
With 30 years in private service, Kellie Geres has become a nanny industry leader who specializes in working with divorced parents; transitioning to household management; and working with nanny organizations and agencies to provide consulting, and small business and social media services.

Kellie has taken her skills and works with the industry organizations APNA and INA by coordinating industry conferences and special projects. In addition, Kellie is the national co-chair for National Nanny Recognition Week, DEMA-DC chapter president, and maintains several industry blogs, including Regarding Nannies and Nanny Trainings.

Kellie was named the 1997 International Nanny Association "Nanny of the Year," and was honored with the Domestic Estate Management Association Lifetime Achievement Award in 2014.

Chapter 18. Separated Families

Kellie has presented programs at several industry events, including Nannypalooza, INA, All Star Nanny Conference, and InterNational Nanny Training Day, and has been interviewed for television, print, and radio.

Kellie resides in the Washington, DC, area. When not wearing her many hats in this industry, she enjoys traveling, reading, and a really good glass of wine.

AllThingsNanny.com

Nanny Basics and Beyond

Chapter 19. Exceptional Children

"Working with a child who struggles to meet even basic milestones gives you a greater appreciation for the importance of those milestones." Tara Lindsay

To better understand the vital role a nanny can play in this type of family, I spoke with Tara Lindsay. Tara has specialized in caring for exceptional children and helps other nannies through these challenging jobs.

In 2017, the U.S. Centers for Disease Control and Prevention* estimated that about 15 percent of the children between the ages of 3 and 17 have developmental disabilities. This does not include chronic illnesses that have no direct effect on learning. So the chances are good that you will care for a child who has nontypical childhood needs at some point in your career.

As a nanny, you might care for a child who experiences allergies, asthma, ADHD (Attention-Deficit Hyperactivity Disorder), Autism Spectrum Disorder, cancer, cerebral palsy, cystic fibrosis, diabetes, digestive problems, Fetal Alcohol Spectrum Disorder, Fragile X syndrome, a heart condition, hearing loss, intellectual disability, kernicterus, muscular dystrophy, Tourette syndrome, sensory problems, and vision impairment. The list can go on and on. Working with an exceptional child might also mean that the child in your care has intelligence way above average. The reality is that any atypical issue that a child could face may categorize the child as "exceptional."

Children who face any of these issues can grow, learn, and succeed in life. Medical advances are made every day that can help them, but they need for more than just their physical requirements to be met. These children need you to want to understand both their uniqueness and their averageness. To help them learn and grow just like their peers. They need for you to take the time to understand what they need to succeed.

The Needs of the Parents

Before you take a job with a parent who has an exceptional child, before you even interview with this type of family, it is important to understand not just what this parent wants from you but what he needs. First and foremost, this parent needs a nanny who is kind, loving, and can see his whole child, not just the child's particular need. You should see beyond the diagnosis to the child inside. You should be able to find unique ways to engage with the child at the child's level.

> "Even in the most challenging situation, you should be someone who can look past the apparent struggles to see the positives and the possibilities."
> Tara Lindsay

Consistency is vital in a home with a child who has exceptional needs. Often even the simplest of activities—an activity that we take for granted—must be regulated and scheduled. It will be necessary that you are able to take the recommendations of doctors and therapists and implement these recommendations in the home and in your daily life. This can be challenging, and you will have to multi-task and find creative solutions.

You need to be willing and eager to learn more about the diagnosis. This might mean that you go out of your way to research on your own or that you attend appointments and treatments so that you can ask questions directly to the people treating the child. You should be a person with a thirst for knowledge who is not only able to understand complex issues but can take that knowledge and implement it in the home, even through difficult circumstances.

While you should be able to work independently and think constructively, you should also be willing and able to follow directions from the parents. Ultimately, while you can suggest new ideas for changing the way you approach the child's situation, it is the parents' decision about what is implemented in the home. Parents with an exceptional child can be very particular about the way things are done. While you might not always agree with the parents, it is your responsibility to not just follow their directions but to do so with excitement and passion.

Do You Have It?

There are certain personality characteristics that will help you in this type of job. It is essential that you have a heart for it. Parents who have an exceptional child do not need someone who is half in the job and half someplace else. If you are going to accept a position like this, you must be committed. This is not a job you should ever take to pad your résumé or just because you don't have any other options. There are so many stressors on these parents; they do not need a nanny who is only half committed and planning to leave when a better job is offered.

Chapter 19. Exceptional Children

You must have excellent communication skills, especially when dealing with documentation. This job will require clear and consistent documentation of activities, from new attempts to medications taken. Even simple things like bowel movements can be noteworthy for children who have exceptional needs, so you need to be able to make detailed and accurate notes.

You will need to be flexible. This means that you should be flexible with the time you can provide to the family. Attending therapy and doctor appointments might be outside your regular work schedule, but it can be critical for you to attend appointments. You might also need to adjust schedules if the child needs to have surgery or go into the hospital. Being available for extra help can relieve part of the pressure that the parent feels during these times. You will also need to be emotionally and mentally flexible. This means that you are able to take in new and sometimes somber information with grace and clarity.

You should have a basic working knowledge of the different developmental milestones that a child will go through, realizing that while a child with special needs might not meet them at the typical time, the child will still work to develop these milestones. The better working knowledge you have of the stages of learning and development, the more easily you can work with the child. It can also help you see areas of development where the child might need additional help. A parent who has a child with an exceptional need tends to be hyper-focused on that obstacle. Missing signs of other problems can be easy. You can help the parent see the child's growth from a different perspective and help guide the parent to seek advice from additional professionals.

It is imperative that you understand what the parent is facing. Even a simple diagnosis of allergies can be devastating to a parent who is faced with a lifetime of caring for and keeping the child safe. It may seem easy to you to adjust to new therapies and appointments, but when you are the parent and all the responsibility falls on you to provide for your child, it can quickly get overwhelming. Having a nanny who can not only see these struggles but in very real ways can relieve some of the stress can be life-changing for the parent.

At the same time, you need to remember that you too have limits on what you are physically, emotionally, and mentally able to do. Don't take on more than you are can. Watch for signs in yourself that you need to take a break or a vacation. The parent in this situation understands all too well the importance of being whole and present. You need to as well.

Challenges

It can be very isolating to work with these families. There are many limitations that you will face when caring for an exceptional child. There might be physical limitations or limits on how much or where the child can go in public. The schedule can be crazy between doctor appointments and therapy visits.

Exhaustion is also a genuine problem for you if you take this type of job. The job might require lifting and moving things that your typical nanny job does not, but it might take a toll on you mentally as well. It can just be so physically and emotionally draining that you don't want to do anything outside of work but sleep. All of this can cause you to begin to be isolated. If you take a job with a child who has exceptional needs, make sure you are not only taking time to rest, but you are also taking time to do things that you enjoy.

At times, dealing with the medical system can be infuriating and heartbreaking. In the US, you can find doctors and specialists to help with everything, but often they provide contradictory information and not all are equally supportive. You can assist families as they navigate the system and find additional support services.

Working with the parents can also be challenging. There can be complications when it comes to sharing information and communicating concerns, and these should be considered and managed carefully. Often a parent relies on you to a greater degree for emotional support. This is another reason that you must be fully committed to the job and emotionally whole. Watching the parent struggle to be heard by doctors, receive the care that is needed, or even get insurance to pay for prescribed medications or treatments can be emotionally challenging for you. It is not possible to take on that much stress without a good support system for yourself. Don't neglect your own needs.

Rewards

While there are challenges to be sure, there are also great rewards in caring for a family with an exceptional child.

"This job will also give you the opportunity to challenge yourself. It will broaden your perspective and knowledge, which will help you grow in your professional career and might help you in positions you have in the future. Learn everything you can about the special needs with which your child is struggling." Tara Lindsay

You may have the chance to develop resources and a network of professionals who you can get to know. As you meet doctors, nurses, and other therapists, keep track of who they are, what they do, and if you found them helpful. It might help you to direct a parent toward the right help in the future, and these individuals can be a place to turn to when you need answers. When you have direct contact with these professionals, they can even provide you with professional references in the future.

Children with typical needs can seem to fly through milestones with ease. Working with an exceptional child will help you come to a more intimate knowledge of development.

Through this job, you will gain a broader perspective of what it means to be successful. Watching a child struggle to do things that come easily to other children will help you to focus on the effort that goes into achieving any goal. The experience will help you to fully understand what it means to work hard and be intentional about your ambitions.

This short story from Emily Perl Kingsley perfectly explains what it is like for a parent to have an exceptional child.

WELCOME TO HOLLAND
By Emily Perl Kingsley (copyright 1987)

I am often asked to describe the experience of raising a child with a disability—to try to help people who have not shared that unique experience to understand it, to imagine how it would feel. It's like this...

When you're going to have a baby, it's like planning a fabulous vacation trip—to Italy. You buy a bunch of guide books and make your wonderful plans. The Coliseum. The Michelangelo David. The gondolas in Venice. You may learn some handy phrases in Italian. It's all very exciting.

After months of eager anticipation, the day finally arrives. You pack your bags and off you go. Several hours later, the plane lands. The stewardess comes in and says, "Welcome to Holland."

"Holland?!?" you say. "What do you mean Holland?? I signed up for Italy! I'm supposed to be in Italy. All my life I've dreamed of going to Italy."

But there's been a change in the flight plan. They've landed in Holland and there you must stay.

The important thing is that they haven't taken you to a horrible, disgusting, filthy place, full of pestilence, famine and disease. It's just a different place.

So you must go out and buy new guide books. And you must learn a whole new language. And you will meet a whole new group of people you would never have met.

It's just a different place. It's slower-paced than Italy, less flashy than Italy. But after you've been there for a while and you catch your breath, you look around...and you begin to notice that Holland has windmills...and Holland has tulips. Holland even has Rembrandts.

But everyone you know is busy coming and going from Italy...and they're all bragging about what a wonderful time they had there. And for the rest of your life, you will say "Yes, that's where I was supposed to go. That's what I had planned."

And the pain of that will never, ever, ever, ever go away...because the loss of that dream is a very, very significant loss.

But...if you spend your life mourning the fact that you didn't get to Italy, you may never be free to enjoy the very special, the very lovely things...about Holland.

There can be such *joy* in this work, but you need to go into it with an open heart and mind, ready to work hard to help the child and parent in need.

TARA LINDSAY

Tara Lindsay has been taking care of other people's children for over 30 years and has worked as a nanny for the past 24 years. Tara attended Central Michigan University, where she studied Special Education and Early Childhood, and then pursued a degree in Public Health Education and Health Promotion. She has cared for children of all ages, stages, and developmental ability levels, as well as worked with a variety of family types. She was trained as a Newborn Care Specialist by the Alexandria School in Solon, Ohio, and has passed the International Nanny Association Nanny Credential Exam. Tara currently is a full-time, live-out nanny for an Oakland County family with three young boys.

Nanny Basics and Beyond

Tara is a Co-Founder and Director of MPNA. At the national level, she has served as Secretary for the Professional Nanny Association and offered advice to nannies and parents as the PNA "Ask Nanny." She has twice been a workshop presenter at Nannypalooza, a national professional education conference, and has been a presenter at local parenting events. Tara volunteers with Be the Match, a division of the National Marrow Donor Program to recruit and educate potential marrow donors. She is on the board of directors for Ryan Rocks Outdoor Adventures, a Michigan-based charity for children with cancer. Tara was named a 2010 Outstanding Young Michigander by the Michigan Jaycees for her numerous volunteer and philanthropic activities, and she served as the 2014 Leadership Consultant for the Wyandotte chapter of the Michigan Jaycees.

Michigan Professional Nanny Association, MichiganProNannies.org

*https://www.cdc.gov/ncbddd/developmen taldisabilities/about.html

Chapter 20. Caring for Multiples

"A nanny who cares for multiples will need to excel at multitasking because in any given five-minute period you will need to meet five different very urgent needs. This will take the ability to think on your feet, do more than one thing at once, and do it all with a smile."
Jenny Brown

I talked with Jenny Brown, a former INA Nanny of the Year and current nanny to triplets, to understand this growing nanny niche a bit better.

Since 1980, with the increase and relative safety of reproductive technologies, the rate of twins or multiples has been climbing in the US and around the world. Chances are that you will care for multiples at some point in your career.

Nanny Basics and Beyond

Having an understanding of how to work with more than one child who is the same age can give you a leg up when you are interviewing for a job.

Advantages

With any niche market in the industry, there will be advantages to working with multiples. In this case, there are several significant advantages to accepting and working in a job with twins or other multiple sets. For starters, the children will always have built-in playmates. Children often complain that they don't have someone to play with, but multiples are natural playmates. They learn from each other and having them working toward milestones around the same time can provide for healthy competition.

> "You will never be bored and will find yourself around happy chaos much of the time." Jenny Brown

If excitement is something that you thrive on, a job with multiples can be a fantastic position for you. There is never a dull moment in a home with multiples, and every event is an adventure.

Typically when you work with multiples, you have a higher compensation rate because it is a more demanding and intense job. Working in this job will also help you build skills and experiences that can be valuable as you look for a job in the future. Even families who do not have multiple children will look at your experience with multiples and think that if you can handle more than one child of the same age, you can handle anything their children will do.

Obstacles

"Think about the number of toys, games, equipment, and supplies that one child normally has today, and then you multiply that by the number of multiples, you will soon find your head spinning." Jenny Brown

Of course, there are also obstacles that you will need to overcome and learn to embrace to do this job effectively. Organizing and keeping track of all the stuff the children have is a challenge. When the children are older, you have sports and other activities that you need to arrange. It is possible to find suitable systems and structures to help. Labeling everything, using color-coding systems, and keeping things easy to find are just a few tips that can help you stay on top of things.

Children who are around each other much of the time often get each other sick. This is true for any family with more than one child, but multiple children seem to do this to a higher degree. It is a recognized fact that children who spend time in close proximity to each other will share germs and illnesses. While it might not be more common with multiples, it certainly feels like it to the caregivers. When a child is sick, he or she can be especially needy. Well, you can imagine how that works when multiples are sick at the same time. It gets even worse when children don't get sick all at the same time because just as one child starts feeling better, another child will start feeling sick. It can seem like a never-ending cycle.

The more children you care for, the more work you will have. Getting lunch on the table for two or more children can take forever. You can solve this problem by involving the children in the activities they can do as early as possible. Organizing the kitchen so that children can get dishes and put them away will not only help you at mealtime but will foster independence and a strong work ethic. Showing the children how to sort dirty laundry and put clean laundry away will, in the long run, help relieve your stress while giving them a sense of accomplishment.

It can be hard to have multiples go through the same phases at the same time. Milestones like potty training times two, three, and more can be a nightmare. On the other hand, having them all pass these milestones close together can help the children who need extra guidance. For instance, when a child who struggles with potty training sees siblings using a toilet, it can help that child to understand what is supposed to be done. There can also be a healthy level of competition with these milestones. When one child in the group can accomplish a task, the others generally want to follow suit.

It can also be a challenge to push back against the notion that twins should dress and act alike. While that may be cute for the occasional picture or event, having the children wear the same outfit all the time can make the children feel like they don't have their own identity. Experts are now warning against continually dressing twins alike and instead allowing them to develop their own sense of self. Twins and multiples will always have a strong connection, and dressing alike will not aid in this bond.

Outings can also be difficult with multiples. Multiplying everything by the number of children you have means that you feel like you are packing for the weekend just to go to the park. Think carefully about what to expect, and research the place where you will be going to make sure you have what you need.

You will need to be sure that you can keep everyone safe and secure. You will always want to keep your eyes on the children, but it can help to practice holding hands with each other or to holding the stroller at all times, so that everyone stays together. You should also talk to the children about your expectations for their behavior before you venture out. This will help them not only have a better understanding of how you plan to keep them safe but it will also help them anticipate what is coming next in their day, so that transitions will be smoother.

Outings with multiples is a bit more like a daycare group going on a field trip than it is for the average nanny, and therefore you need to act more like a field trip supervisor. When you take one child to the zoo, you can go where that child wants to go pretty much all of the time. However, when you go on an outing with multiples, you need to work as a group, stopping more often to use the potty and letting everyone choose an activity.

Sibling fights also look a little different with multiples. While multiples might not fight more than other siblings, arguments between multiples are unique. When siblings who are different ages fight, there is usually one with more power who has control over the situation. While this can be true with multiples, it is not always so obvious.

Personality

As I said before, a job with multiples is not a perfect fit for every nanny. If you are considering taking a job with twins or other multiples, there are certain personality traits that will be beneficial to you.

Every job caring for children takes patience, but a job working with multiples needs a triple shot. Take the example of an outing. Every time you go someplace you are dealing with multiple

Chapter 20. Caring for Multiples

individual human beings. They each have
different likes and needs at different times. So
when one is hungry, another will probably need
to use the bathroom. While one wants to take a
walk to the park, the other will want to collect
leaves across the street. It takes an enormous
amount of patience and daily endurance to help
these children navigate their disagreements.

You will also need to be flexible. While it is
important to plan outings, you also need to be
prepared for the many changes to the plan that
will come your way. You are after all meeting the
needs of not just one other person but many,
and that might divert you from your original
plan. Being flexible with a positive attitude will
help the children feel safe because they will
know that no matter what their needs are, you
are there to meet them. This flexibility will also
help the children learn to be more comfortable
when plans change. In the long run, flexibility
will benefit the parents, children, and caregiver.

You need to be the kind of person who can
not only come up with and implement systems
to help make life more comfortable, but you also
need to be able to adjust these systems as the
children grow. You will need to find creative
ways to support the children as they learn these
practices. The follow-through will be a challenge
when you have several children who you are
trying to discipline at the same time.
Consistency will be important. A stable routine
with the children will be a tremendous asset.

309

Above all else, you need to have a passion for the work. This is not an easy job. There will be days that you don't get to sit down much, but each and every day will be an adventure. If you have a passion for the job you are doing, you will love every day.

Making Yourself an Expert

While it is possible to land a job working with multiples without much experience, many families who have multiples or are going to have them will be less likely to hire you if you don't have experience.

If you don't have experience working with multiples, you could start building volunteer experience. Working in a local preschool, perhaps your religious children's program or even the local community center playgroup can help you gain exposure to children who are around the same age. You could also work in a "nanny share" as well. In a "nanny share," you work with two families, usually in the home of one of the families and often with children who are close in age. While it is not precisely a multiples position, many of the practices will be the same.

Lots of areas have "twin" groups that you could reach out to with an offer to volunteer for an upcoming event to gain experience. Doing this can help very appreciative parents, while at the same time help you achieve the skills that

Chapter 20. Caring for Multiples

you will need on a résumé. Be sure to ask for a written reference if you do this.

If you know someone with multiples, you could even volunteer to care for those children free of charge to gain experience. Families with multiples often cannot afford to hire a nanny or even babysitter. They might be willing to exchange the service of taking care of their children for a few hours a week for a recommendation letter for future job searches. Be sure to clarify how long you are willing to do this.

You can also take courses and continuing education related to working with multiples. At local, national, and international nanny conferences there may be workshops dealing with the topic. Then, when you are ready to apply for a job with multiples, you will want to highlight these particular classes to the parent. Showing that you have gone out of your way to gain a new experience will send the parent a big message.

When you interview for a job working with multiples, ask the thoughtful questions that send the message that you understand the unique challenges that caregivers of multiples face. Ask about specific schedules and routines that the children have and how they cooperate through those. Be sure to ask about each child's unique personality and what types of rewards and consequences might be most effective for each. Showing that you see the children as individuals is crucial.

With the rise in multiple births, this is a growing niche for nannies who have a passion for adventure and excitement. If you are lucky enough to work with these wonderful children, enjoy the time and make it fun.

JENNY BROWN

A professional nanny for 24 years, Jenny Brown loves her chosen career. She was truly honored when she was named the 2005 International Nanny Association's Nanny of the Year award. Jenny has been incredibly fortunate to work with amazing families and children. She loves being with a family from the early days and has been fortunate to continue on until the children begin their elementary school experience. She has especially loved her time and accomplishments working with multiples, including twins and triplets.

For many years, Jenny led her local nanny support group, Northwest Nanny Association. Through this organization she has arranged and participated in volunteer opportunities with several charitable organizations for families and children. Jenny has written numerous articles for her former nanny newsletter, and she has been interviewed for newspaper articles relating to the nanny industry. She loves planning and hosting learning opportunities for her local area nannies, including National Nanny Training Day from its inception in 2012. Jenny has a passion for this industry and is a dynamic representation of a professional nanny.

NorthwestNannyAssocation.com

Nanny Basics and Beyond

Chapter 21. Working with Teens

"Love, understanding, and consistency are vital to providing teens with the stability that they too often pretend they don't need. The relationship they have with you and their parents forms the foundation of all other relationships."
Carli Lintemuth

To help us appreciate the often misunderstood role a nanny takes in the lives of teens, I talked with Carli Lintemuth, who is a nanny for teens in Michigan.

When most people hear the word "nanny," they think of someone working with young children. However, that is not always the case. Many nannies work with a family that has children who are older and even well into their

Nanny Basics and Beyond

teens. The role of the nanny changes significantly as children age. The daily conversations that you have with a toddler are very different from those that you will have with a 13-year-old. However, those talks with a teenager are just as vital to that young person's well-being and growth.

The process of building self-reliance in teens is a hurdle in today's world. Many young adults are leaving their home for college or a career with limited life skills. How can a nanny foster a sense of independence while still caring for the child?

Basic Needs

"You can't coddle them like a child, but, at the same time, their brains aren't fully formed like an adult's. Their bodies might look like an adult's, but they are still impulsive." Carli Lintemuth

One of the most significant challenges in caring for teens is recognizing the complexity of these maturing humans. A major role of caring for a teen is trying to find a way to meet their basic needs but also help them to become independent. Soon they will be leaving the comfort of their parents' home, and they will need to know how to do things like wash their clothes, pay bills, save money, and be on time. When parents and caregivers do all these things

316

for teens or even fight with them to accomplish these tasks, the teens are not building any responsibility for their own lives. When you solve all the problems that teens face, they do not grow to be stable and secure. When teens are not required to fix mistakes that they create, they do not learn courtesy and respect for their belongings and other people.

These habits must grow little by little, and preparation should start when they are much younger than 13. However, even if you find yourself caring for teens who have every problem solved for them, are not required to fix their own mistakes, or are unable to complete tasks on still own, you will still need to start someplace.

That start can be to let the teens keep track of their schedules, homework, and responsibilities. Set up a well-organized calendar and teach the teens how to do this on their own. Teens usually love technology, and, in this circumstance, technology can be their friend. Using apps to stay connected will help the teens not only keep track of a schedule and learn to be responsible for themselves but also allow them to stay connected with you and their parents. Sending silly memes, funny pictures, or cute videos that you know they would like will help the teens feel loved and special.

Emotional Investment

While caring for children in their teens and tweens brings with it tasks like carpooling, preparing meals, homework help, and making sure they do their household chores, your most significant role is to be emotionally invested in them. They need a safe place to fall. Often they don't feel that their parents can be there for them anymore. You need to be that place for them.

Listening is a critical part of this. Even when the topics they are talking about may seem unimportant to you, you need to listen. Issues that you think are insignificant, to teens, may be the only things they can think about. Half-listening, responding in platitudes, or blowing them off sends the message that you are not really interested in what matters to them.

Detachment from Parents

Many parents who have a nanny for their teen want more than someone to drive their child from one destination to the next. Parents want someone who their teen respects and in whom the teen can confide.

One of the challenges of working with teens revolves around your off hours. It is difficult and at times hurtful to have to tell teens that they cannot reach out to you when you are not "on the clock." Being willing to take text messages or phone calls in your off hours can provide the teens the safe cushion to feel independent from their parents but not be left to do things that are unsafe.

Chapter 21. Working with Teens

You may find the best way to support the family is to be that mentor for the teens as they transition away from needing constant care from parents. It is absolutely essential that before you begin to allow the teens in your care to confide in you, you come to a mutual understanding with their parents in writing. Does your employer expect you to share all the information the teens disclose or is she willing to allow you to use your judgment regarding what you disclose to her? Whatever the parent's decision on this is, you need to respect and uphold it.

It is your job to protect the teens and sometimes that means passing information to the parent, and sometimes it means helping the teens find a way to tell the parent on their own. You can be a sounding board to help the teens find the words to share the story with their parent. Doing this can help teens make an informed and mature decision in the situation and aid in the communication with their parent.

Example:
The 17-year-old you care for has come home past curfew. The parent is angry. The teen is angry because she wasn't "that" late. She feels that her parent is overreacting, that he treats her like a child, and he is being unfair. You are a safe place for the 17-year-old to turn. She confides in you about this unjust situation. You can say something like:

"That sounds like a rough argument. I'm so sorry that happened. However, when a friend and I are meeting up, if she's not there at the time we agreed on, I start to worry that something terrible has happened. I would imagine that feeling is multiplied when it's your child who is late. I know your parents were mad at you but understand that anger was actually worrying. Your parents were scared, and that's how their fear came out. I promise you that this is going to happen again. What if you had a conversation ahead of time to try and prevent the outcome? You could say 'I know I was late. I am sorry. Maybe in the future, I can call or text you if I am running late, so you don't worry. Then I can explain the circumstances to you.' If you called *before you were late* and explained to your parents that you are safe but you are running late and you are trying to get home as soon as you can, at least your parents would not be worried about you. I think it would also make your parents feel good that you're admitting you screwed up and feel bad about it. You know why they are mad and you're trying really hard not to scare them again."

Safety

Keeping children safe is an essential responsibility of yours. This role changes when the children get older. When children are young, we focus on personal safety, things like not running into the street, avoiding things that are

Chapter 21. Working with Teens

hot, not talking to people who are unsafe, or even what to do if you are bullied. When you work with teens and tweens, you are still trying to keep the teens safe, but now it is in a different way, because today's teens have to deal with sex, drugs, drinking, date rape, and cyberbullying.

Have frank and honest discussions about these safety issues with teens.

"The teens need to know that you're not a stupid adult with your head in the sand. You know what is going on and you are paying attention to what happens to them." Carli Lintemuth

Cyber safety is a huge part of caring for teens. Cyberbullying is so prevalent, so being a part of their digital world can help you spot red flags. You will want to watch for signs that they are being bullied or that they are bullying others. Follow them on social media and point out posts that might not be wise. It is necessary to keep up-to-date with the latest trending topics so that you can discuss those topics with them. You can point out news stories where someone was hurt by something posted online. Many teens don't truly understand the reach of social media and what it can do to a person if they say or post the wrong thing. They also don't recognize that the quick message they think will go only to someone they think of as a friend will likely end up in the hands of many other people.

Another big part of safety for teens is security in their independence. It is wise to make sure that teens tell you where they are at all times. Not to be nosey, but in case there was ever an emergency. You need to know how to get ahold of them. Children who are now teens were babies before 9/11. They don't remember the panic the world felt, and they cannot grasp what it would feel like to be unable to get help until it is too late. It is your job to help them understand this reality.

There might be times that teens let you know where they are but do not tell their parent. You will have to speak with the parents ahead of time and judge what is important to share with parents and what can be kept to yourself. If you can work out an understanding with the parents that you will share details when it is necessary but that allowing the teens to have this buffer zone will build independence, the teens will be more willing to share those details with you and not their parents. Of course, you should never withhold important information from the parents.

It is important to discuss their personal safety when the teens are not with you. Use a lot of "what ifs" in your conversations. What if your car breaks down in a place where there are not many people? What if you are with friends and you think someone is following you? What if you come home, the door is open, and it seems like someone is in the house? What if you are at a party and you think someone put something in your drink? What if you are walking home and someone grabs you? These are tough questions, but a teenager should be able to discuss them with you. You can even let the teens come up with their own scenarios. They will feel more empowered when they figure out possible solutions to these problems and will be more likely to be able to actively problem-solve if the worst does happen.

Have conversations about world safety too. Help them fill and keep a backpack supplied for an emergency in their car. Talk to them about school shootings or shootings in other public places. Ask them to consider what they would do to stay safe in their school, in the mall, at a coffee shop, at work, or wherever they spend time.

It might be a good idea to take a few self-defense classes with your teen. Everyone can benefit from knowing basic self-defense moves, and if the teens take the course with you, they might feel less intimidated by the concept of a physical confrontation. Self-defense skills can not only be skills that could save their life, but the knowledge that they can be proactive can be a confidence booster in teens who are less secure in themselves.

Mediation

Often your role in the home with teens is the mediator between parent and teen. You don't want to share details of the day in front of children, especially teens, so sending a text message to the parent before she arrives home at the end of the day can be a way to give her a heads up to what she has waiting for her. If something terrible has happened during the day, a text can be a good way to share the information with the parent and allow her to prepare her reaction and be ready to respond in an uplifting way, as opposed to the parent walking in the door at the end of a long day to bad news.

Scenario 1: A 15-year-old boy has failed a test. He is devastated. The parent comes home after a difficult day. She is agitated in general from the day, and then she hears about the failed test and explodes in frustration, making the situation so much worse.

Scenario 2: When the teen comes home and shares the details about the failed test, you email or text the parent, letting her know that the boy has had a miserable day because he failed his test. He is so worried and is a real mess. You tell her that you wanted her to know before she got home. Now the mom is not caught off guard with the news. She has a better chance to put aside the stress from her day and think ahead about how to react when the child "breaks" the news about the failed test. This

Chapter 21. Working with Teens

allows for an entirely different outcome for the whole evening, and it preserves the relationship the parent has with her teen.

In the Scenario 1, the mom feels like she is having a horrible day too. The stress from work seems like it followed her home and because she reacted in the way she did, she may feel guilty. Then, not only is the child dealing with the consequences of failing the test, he also must endure the explosive reaction from his parent. He starts thinking, "Should I have lied about the grade? Does his parent think he is stupid?" None of that was intended by the parent. The parent was just overwhelmed by the day in general. Undoubtedly this can create a lot of unintended stress in the parent-child relationship that can be hard to repair.

However, in the second scenario, you were able to prevent or at least minimize all of that. The parent had a chance to take a breath and have a smoother transition from work to home. Since there was no emotional blow-up, instead of the boy questioning his relationship with his mother, he comes out feeling more connected with her. It reinforces his trust in his parent.

Being a nanny for teens is not an easy task. Whether the child has grown into adolescence before your very eyes or you have taken the job caring for the teen relatively recently, the relationship you have with the child is built on trust, excellent communication, and reliability. Often you are less of a nanny and more of a mentor. Finding the right balance of care while empowering teens to gain freedom is vital to the success of the relationship. Teens will only learn to respect you when you learn to respect them.

CARLI LINTEMUTH

Carli Lintemuth has been a professional nanny in the metro Detroit area for over 20 years, with the last eight years focused on working with teenagers. She is currently training to be a Newborn Care Specialist, and serves the International Nanny Association as an INA Ambassador as well as a part of the nominations committee.

Chapter 22. Traveling with Families

"'Seeing the world' looks very different when you are the main caregiver for the children." Helen McCarthy

To help with this very common experience, I talked with Helen McCarthy of Top Baby Guru about her experience traveling with children.

Working for a family who travels might sound like an exhilarating adventure. You may dream of seeing the world, experiencing different cultures, meeting new people, all while you work. The reality can be far from what you have imagined. As a traveling nanny, you need to have the right skills, as well as the understanding that while you may be traveling the world, you will likely spend most of your time in hotel rooms and airports with tired, cranky children.

> "The best part about traveling with children is you get to see many parts of the world you may never have seen before, spending time with your charges in different places that are not the normal four walls of your workplace."
> Helen McCarthy

Setting Up the Work Agreement

Nannies who travel with families fall into two separate categories. Some nannies have found a specialized niche called "traveling nannies." If you are a traveling nanny, you are hired for short periods of time to take a trip with the family, stay with the children while parents travel, or transport children from one place to another. It will take years to prepare for this specialty. Often a parent who is looking for a traveling nanny wants someone with a lot of travel experience. You could also be a full-time nanny who works for parents who travel often and usually expects the nanny to accompany them on these trips.

If you know that a family you are about to take a job with will be traveling a lot, make sure that you include details about this in a work agreement from the start. If the family you are working for suddenly asks you to take a trip, make sure that before you say yes, you add extra details to your work agreement so that there are no surprises along the way.

Include in the work agreement:

What is your hourly rate while on this trip? Many families will try to tell you that they are giving you vacation and therefore try to pay you less than your regular hourly rate. However, the reality is that a job traveling with a family is much harder than a job in the children's home. Don't sell yourself short and take a pay cut to get a vacation. Chances are you will not be vacationing as much as you think you will.

Who pays for everything and how payment will be made? For instance, items like hotel, airfare, and other transportation are normally paid directly by the parents, but how much are they paying of your food, activities, and other discretionary funds?

- Will you be reimbursed for food and activities with the children, or given cash as needed?
- Do you have a credit card that you can use for these needs?
- Are expenses outside of the time you care for children included?
- Since you do not have the regular transportation that you do at home, will they be helping you pay for personal transit when needed?

- Are they going to pay for any of your "off hours" activities? Most parents expect you to cover those costs on your own, but being clear about the costs that you will incur is critical to have in the work agreement.

What activities will you and the children be participating in with the family? Do the parents want you to stay in the hotel with the children while they see the sights?

- Do they want you to come along with the family while everyone sees the sights?
- Do they want you to step out on your own with the children to see the locations?
- Do they want to take their children off on their own without you for a while?

Maybe it is a balance of all of these. Discuss and get in writing their expectations of you before you leave.

What are the sleeping arrangements while traveling?

- Will you have your own room or are you sleeping in the room with the children?
- If you are sleeping in the room with the children, be sure that you are paid for sleeping, because those are working hours.

When and how much time off do you have? Unless being well compensated for it, you should not be expected to work 24/7. You should expect some downtime each week.

Chapter 22. Traveling with Families

What kind of communication will you be able to expect? Traveling means that you don't always have the same reliable technology. If you are traveling a lot with the family, you have an expectation to communicate with the outside world. Discuss how the parent can help you make this happen. You might request a cell phone that works in whatever place you travel to or a prepaid phone card so you can call internationally from landlines when needed. Have a plan so that you will always be able to communicate with the outside world.

How will you communicate with your employers while you travel and are not together? You will want to have a plan for getting in touch with the parents of the children you are caring for if they are out for the day and you are with the children. It might not be as simple as it is when you are at home.

If traveling over a holiday, what will the holiday schedule be like? Will you be on duty or off? Can you or will you be expected to join the family in the celebration?

Benefits of Traveling with the Family

There can be real perks to traveling with the family. The first is the experience. Just the act of navigating the traveling experience with a family is a valuable adventure. It takes time to perfect this art. Things that you are good at when traveling by yourself become more complicated when children are involved. How many diapers will we need before we get our large suitcases back and what happens if our luggage is lost? You don't want to take so much that your luggage becomes cumbersome but you also want to make sure that you have enough supplies to last even if there are delays. These are valuable experiences that translate not only to other jobs where you will travel but will help you in any position you might have later in your career.

While it is true that you will likely not see as much of the locations that you travel to as you would if you were merely a tourist, you do get to spend time in other places. If you can negotiate time off to see the sights into a work agreement, you will at least be able to experience the sights that are the most important to you. Depending on the ages of the children you are caring for, you might be able to experience new places with the children.

Often, traveling with a family means that you will stay at hotels and visit locations that you normally could not afford if you were going on your own. Five-star resorts, private islands, and historic castles are all locations where nannies have been known to stay while visiting with families.

It can be pretty amazing to see and explore the world with the children in your care. Learning about new cultures alongside them helps you to see the world from a whole new point of view.

Chapter 22. Traveling with Families

Challenges of Traveling with a Family

Traveling with a family is not right for everyone. While there are fantastic benefits, there are also challenges you need to anticipate when you travel with a family. You will likely be working long hours, and that might be isolating. Communication when traveling out of your country can be difficult. Even connecting with friends and family can be a challenge. Many nannies go into a travel job thinking that they are getting paid to go on vacation, but the reality is that this is not *your* vacation. It is work for you, and you should never lose sight of that.

You may be away from your home for long periods of time. This can be very hard if you are married, have a partner, or have your own children. You need to set up the expectations of those who count on you being around so your personal relationships stay healthy. Taking a job where you travel might mean that you don't spend holidays with friends and family. You may not have as much time with them as you would like. Protect yourself by knowing your boundaries.

You may find that the most challenging part of traveling as a nanny is living out of a suitcase for weeks and months. Having to be selective about what you pack and what you don't pack, wearing the same few items of clothes for weeks at a time, being careful about what souvenirs you purchase to take home—all are routines that will seem odd at first but with which you will soon become accustomed.

Difficult Situations

There are always surprises when you travel, especially when you are with children. Delays, lost luggage, and dealing with different time zones are minor inconveniences when you are by yourself but can quickly become a nightmare with children. When you travel with children, you need to learn to think ahead—way ahead. You also need to develop creative problem-solving skills. That might mean that you have to walk up to a stranger and ask for a diaper because you used your last one three hours ago. It could mean that you need to smooth things over with the passenger in front of you because the three-year-old you have been traveling with has been kicking her chair for the last two hours. It might mean that you need to invent new games that you have not played before because the tablet that you brought for the seven-year-old has died, or you need to figure out how much freedom to give an 11-year-old who has traveled more than you.

It might even mean, as in Helen's case, that you need to find a way to convince a security guard to allow the baby to stay asleep through security. Here is her story.

"I was traveling with a young baby, mum, dad, and older sibling. When we were going through security for the return flight, they

Chapter 22. Traveling with Families

decided that a double mountain buggy which had a sleeping baby in it needed to be folded and go through the scanner. Well, of course, everyone knows how big that buggy is, and it would not fit through. Mum, dad, and toddler had gone, through leaving me with baby and buggy and a guard who was at this point shouting at me to remove the baby and fold the buggy. I replied 'No,'; I was not going to wake the baby and the buggy would not fit. He insisted, but I did not want a screaming baby and a broken buggy, so I calmly asked him for his supervisor, who came over and asked what the fuss was about. When the supervisor saw the buggy and the sleeping baby, he waved us through."

While I encourage everyone to follow the directions of the TSA and other security personnel, sometimes a cool but persistent approach to a stressful situation can soothe the tension and work out well in the end.

Be Prepared

Sometimes it is tough to know how to balance being prepared for anything when traveling with children, so you do not need to lug too much around, and packing light. If you are going to be in one location for a while, you can mail supplies ahead. Shipping can be cheaper than checking bags, and if you have time and can plan, this can help.

Nanny Basics and Beyond

You should also do research about the place where you are traveling: the climate, what stores are around, and things that you might be able to purchase locally and therefore not need to bring. This includes where the nearest hospitals, doctors, and pharmacies are located. There may even be some medications that you cannot take into certain countries. Doing your research can save you time down the road.

When traveling with children who are old enough, the children should pack and carry their own travel bag. You will want to help younger children think through what they should bring and what they will need, but they can and should carry their bags as much as possible.

You can also utilize the millions of travel gadgets and supplies that help people pack light. New options come out all the time, so do a little research, talk to other nannies who travel, and find what works for you.

Other Tips

When packing toys and games, avoid those with lots of pieces. When traveling, parts of toys can get lost. That ten-piece puzzle is frustrating with only eight pieces left, and who wants to be crawling around on the floor of the plane looking for the tiny missing pieces of the doll's tea set the six-year-old just had to bring? Leave delicate and multi-part things at home or keep them in baggies stowed away until you are off the plane.

Chapter 22. Traveling with Families

Make sure you leave extra time between flights. When you are traveling alone, a short layover might be ideal, but when you are going with children, you need a little extra time, especially if you have to get through customs.

Pack extra wipes. They come in handy for a lot of situations.

Know what the regulations are on traveling with baby food, breastmilk, or formula. These regulations frequently change so assume nothing. Check again. You don't want to get to the airport and have to throw away a day's worth of food for the children.

Pack healthy, bite-sized snacks that are for the plane only. Chewing helps elevate the pressure in your ears and gives the children something to look forward to.

Let this be the time they don't go screen free. While many parents rightfully want to limit screens at home, traveling is difficult for children. For many parents, this can be the one time when they loosen that regulation. If you don't want to purchase a tablet just for this trip, libraries will rent them for weeks at a time. They come preloaded with educational games and movies.

Find the "kid zone." In most airports, there is a child play area. It might be a little walk to get to but giving your children a place to run around freely will help everyone. If nothing else, young children are fascinated by the moving walkways.

Nanny Basics and Beyond

Traveling with a family can be fun. Prepare for everything you can and then roll with the surprises.

HELEN MCCARTHY

Helen was awarded the title of International Nanny of the Year 2016 by the International Nanny Association.

She is NNEB qualified and has been in the nanny industry for over 27 years.

Helen's main focus is now newborns and, as one of the pre-eminent maternity nurses, she has amassed a deep understanding of the needs and development of newborns, including premature infants, twins, triplets, and babies with allergies.

Helen is the founder of Top Baby Guru and UK Nanny Ltd. She organizes local events and The Great British Nanny Conference, which is held every October in the UK.

In May 2018, Helen was enrolled onto the Board of Directors of The International Nanny Association at its annual conference in Tucson, Arizona.

TopBabyGuru.com
UKNanny.org

Nanny Basics and Beyond

Traveling with a family can be fun. Prepare for everything you can and then roll with the surprises.

HELEN MCCARTHY

Helen was awarded the title of International Nanny of the Year 2016 by the International Nanny Association.

She is NNEB qualified and has been in the nanny industry for over 27 years.

Helen's main focus is now newborns and, as one of the pre-eminent maternity nurses, she has amassed a deep understanding of the needs and development of newborns, including premature infants, twins, triplets, and babies with allergies.

Helen is the founder of Top Baby Guru and UK Nanny Ltd. She organizes local events and The Great British Nanny Conference, which is held every October in the UK.

In May 2018, Helen was enrolled onto the Board of Directors of The International Nanny Association at its annual conference in Tucson, Arizona.

TopBabyGuru.com
UKNanny.org

338

Chapter 23. The In-Home Parent

"With the right family, the right communication, and the right amount of work, you can turn a difficult situation into your 'unicorn family.'"
Marcia Hall

Working in a home where one or both of the parents are home for a significant amount of the time is a challenge for many nannies. You may be hesitant to accept a position where there is a work-from-home parent or a parent who is not working much of the time you are on the clock. However, with the advancements in technology, there lots of benefits for parents who work remotely and many are choosing to do so. As this trend continues to grow, it will be harder and harder to avoid these jobs. You can make it work and it might end up being the perfect job for you.

You do not need to fear this situation. It is possible to care for children in union with the parents who are home most of the time. In fact, many nannies have found such happiness with the situation that they now prefer it.

Ground rules should be worked out with the parent at home before the job begins. These rules apply to the parent, the children, and you. Each party should keep the harmony of the whole house in mind at each step.

You need to understand the motivation and pressure of the parent working from home. Working from home can be a huge benefit for parents because they eliminate their commute, saving on gas, stress, and time. It also means that they spend less time in the morning getting ready for work and that they can still complete projects around the house as they are working, like accepting packages, getting dinner ready, or other tasks. They may work from home because they own their own company and use their house as their office to save money on renting space.

The parent most likely works from home so he can spend more time with his children. Saving time by not going into an office gives him that time back with his children. A parent who is motivated by this desire typically wants to have time throughout the day with his children. This means he might expect you to do other household tasks at particular intervals in the day.

This is where the situation can get complicated and might be why you don't want to work for a parent who is at home. With the right tips and tricks, you can make it work.

Schedule

Start with a basic schedule of the day. Routine gives children a sense of stability and safety. Their brains can only understand and predict a small amount of data. If the children are always trying to determine what comes next in their day, they have less time for learning and growing in new ways. Giving the children the peace of having a basic schedule that is consistent most of the time can help children thrive.

Some children struggle more than others when they don't have a routine or their routine is changed. As children grow, it is helpful to provide sporadic moments when their routine changes. It is healthy for them to learn to adjust to changes in routine, but the more of these moments there are, the less they can master other tasks. When significant stressors are happening in the children's lives (like getting a new caregiver), establishing routines are even more critical.

So talking to the parent who is at home at the beginning of employment regarding your goal to set expectations and routines within the home is vital. Schedule regular events like school pick up, mini visits with the parent and other short visits or activities the parent want to be involved in. Is mom breastfeeding the baby and how does she want to handle those visits?

Often, parents are not able to predict at what point in the day they will emerge from their office and want to spend time with a child. This can provide a challenge to both you and child, but there are ways to still ensure stability for the children. In cases like this, it is best to ask the parent to send a text or call when he will be taking a work break. This way, you can prepare the children to expect a break from your activity.

Once you have this schedule, provide a visual for the children, so they know when the parent will be "away" and when he will be with them. A simple way to mark this can be a simple circle that you put on the fridge or wall. On one side it has a picture of the parent working and on the other it has a picture of the parent playing with the children. Whichever one is up is what is happening. If you have children who need help with the transition, you can also create a "SOON" section of the circle indicating that the parent will be with them soon.

For older children, you could use a clock that shows when the parent will be able to spend time with them. This can help older children begin to tell time and give them a time reference for when they will be the parent next.

Chapter 23. The In-Home Parent

What Should You Do?

A parent may want to spend this time with his children on his own. This means that he would like you to not be present during his time with his children. Another parent might want you to be around for various reasons. For the children, a mixture of both of these can be valuable. It is good for them to see you and their parent interacting in an informal manner.

Knowing when the parent wants you to hang out and when he wants to have one-to-one time with his children can mean the difference between a lighthearted moment together or a chaotic disaster.

The best solution is to find a balance. Spend the first part of this time with parent and children, sharing positive details about the day so far. Then about halfway through, let them know that you are going to get some things done. You could use this opportunity to work on the children's laundry, dishes, or other tidying up work. Maybe the parent wants you to have a little break, and you could check personal messages and social media during this time or read a book. Discuss the different ideas with the parent.

Your return to the group is the first indication for the children that their time with the parent is coming to a close. When you get back to the group, set a timer for the children so they are able to judge how much time is left. This can help the parent too, because he does not have to keep looking at a clock or risk losing track of time.

Return to Work

The transition for the parent to go back to work can often be much harder than having him appear from the office. It is essential to set up expectations for this too. Explain to the parent that lingering during "goodbyes" does more harm than good. Lingering fuels the emotions, giving power to their negative actions in a way that can cause problems.

You need to understand that the parent is worried that the children will feel abandoned by his leaving. Help the parent understand that the reality is that this process is actually beneficial for children. The children need to see that people leave and come back. Sometimes they need to experience this over and over again before they understand it.

The parent might also be hesitant to leave because he is worried that you do not want to or cannot handle dealing with intense emotions from the children. You can put his mind at ease by reminding him that you have everything under control. You are going to provide excellent care for his children. Talk about the activities you have planned for the rest of the day. This can help the parent and the children. Most of all talk about how you understand the children might feel worried, but that they will be back together very soon.

Chapter 23. The In-Home Parent

Help the parent and children to develop a short and simple goodbye routine. It could be a distinctive hug or kiss. It could be special words that are only said when saying goodbye to go to work. Something that the parent and children can come to expect that will reassure the children and remind them that their parent will be back soon.

Other Contact

Children tend to play the "who is going to say yes" game with parents and caregivers. This can be a big problem when parents are at home, especially if the parent wants to have an "open door" policy with his children. It is best to request that the parent not have this policy but instead set up a system where if there is something that the children need, you will reach out to him the same way you would if he was out of the home. Phone, text or even an intercom can work. Whatever is selected should be a method that takes the face-to-face and instant gratification out of the situation.

Once that system is set up, it is imperative that everyone support it. You may be hesitant to request that parents protect your authority in the situation, but it is vital that they do. Children can quickly sense when one adult will be more willing to give in to a situation and they will use that to their advantage.

You can help the children understand when it is appropriate to reach out to their parent by

making a list of situations that might occur and determining for when the parent will be consulted. This can help not only the children understand your authority but it can clarify the parent's expectations as well.

Conflicts

A difference of opinion between you and the parent will happen on every job. It will occur much more frequently when the parent is at home. It is important to state up front the expectation that these disagreements should be avoided in front of the children. Formulate a plan so that when the parent disagrees with your approach to a problem, he can let you know outside of the situation. Request the chance to do the same for him.

Set a good example for children in conflict. If the parent sets a rule or provides discipline, you should 100 percent follow through. This shows the parent that you are a team player and it shows the children that you are united in their best interest.

You may find it hard to advocate for your authority in this same way. It feels awkward to say, "Please don't disagree with me in front of your children." Instead, you could say:

"I know that you will not love and approve of every decision I make when it comes to discipline and caring for your children. I want to receive this feedback from you. However, in order for your child to trust my authority to protect him, he needs to see that you have confidence in my abilities. If you would like me to handle a situation differently in the future, can you send me an email or write me a message about it? We can follow up privately so that I can understand how you would like me to respond in the future."

Know when to Get Out of the House

There are going to be days when the children need time away from the house. This can be an excellent time to set out on an adventure. Take a walk, go to a museum, play at the park. Do something to take the temptation and frustration away from the children.

Talk with the parent about the signs you notice telling you that children might need a fun trip. Ask the parent to look for these signs too. You can even suggest that if he has a particularly important phone call or visitor, he let you know and you can plan to go on an adventure with the children.

While working for a parent who is home a majority of the time can be a challenge, it can also give you a great deal of flexibility. At home, parents are much more likely to give you time off so you can take care of personal needs in the middle of the day. With the right family, the right communication, and the right amount of work, you can turn a difficult situation into your ideal family.

Nanny Basics and Beyond

Chapter 24. Leaving a Job with Grace

"Nannies have every right to their feelings, but they have to deal with them in a constructive, positive way. Love looks forward but hate looks back. We need to continue to move forward."
Glenda Propst

Glenda Propst spoke with me again about this topic. As founder of Nanny Transitions, she has counseled many nannies through the difficult growth that comes when they leave a job.

It is inevitable. At some point in your career, you will leave a nanny job. You may be fortunate to go at the time of your choosing; you might have the family decide for you; it could be that the children have simply outgrown you—but it will happen. The only question is, how will you handle the situation? What steps will you take to ensure that the transition for the children is smooth, and how will you say goodbye?

Knowing that it is Ending

There are telltale signs that a job is coming to an end. One is that you and your employer stop communicating. This relationship is built on mutual trust, respect, and communication. When the communication stops, often the respect and trust fall away too. Not every job where communication has lacked is in danger of ending, but when the parties stop wanting to communicate, there is a danger.

You might sense that you are no longer part of a parenting team. You may feel out of the loop and suddenly are being left out of decisions. Maybe the parent is taking on responsibilities for which you were once responsible. These are all signs that the end could be near.

If you feel that you cannot do anything right for your employer or your employer cannot do anything right for you, this too is a sign. You may stop being patient with each other or cease trying to work through the problems but instead just criticize each other. Maybe you have been hypercritical of your employer's parenting skills, or your employer has complained that the children's laundry has been folded wrong.

"If money has become the driving factor on why you are staying in the job, you need to address the situation. If you want to make the relationship work, then these signs should lead you to a frank conversation with your employer, but if you are ready to leave, then there is a right way to do it." Glenda Propst

Preparing Yourself to Leave

When you can sense the end is coming, you need to get yourself ready for the inevitable. No matter how it happens, don't panic. You need to have a backup plan in place. Financial experts say that it is best to have three months' worth of savings available when you lose a job, so that you know you can carefully look for your next position. If you are a live-in nanny, you should have a place to live lined up. In fact, you should always be prepared for this if you are a live-in nanny because in most states you are an at-will employee and, truthfully, can be let go at any point. Know where you can go in an emergency.

It is always good to keep your résumé up-to-date at all times so that if you need it, you won't panic. Gather the current contact information for your references, get new letters of recommendation, and make sure you have all past evaluations from your current employer. Be careful not to take actions that will startle your current employer and make her take notice. You don't want to be fired before you are prepared to leave.

Nanny Basics and Beyond

It is usually possible to look for a new job before you leave your current position, but it can be hard to schedule interviews while you are working full time. It also can be tricky telling potential employers why you want to leave your current job. Often potential employers want to speak with your latest employer. A professional nanny should always be honest but also focused on the positive and constructive points. Explaining why you are unhappy becomes more of a challenge when you are still in the situation. Some agencies will not work with you if you are currently in a full-time position. This is especially true if you want to work with the agency that placed you in your current job. It puts the agency in the tricky position of supporting you while having an obligation to the family as its client.

Even if you are not planning on looking for your next job while you are still in your current position, you should reconnect with agencies that you have used in the past. Keeping a good relationship with your nanny agency can mean a shorter time between jobs.

Preparing the Children

When it comes to preparing the children for the possibility of leaving, you need to find a balance between sharing too much and not enough. Losing people is a part of growing up and can be looked at as a learning experience. There are ways to help the children understand

352

Chapter 24. Leaving a Job with Grace

that it is OK to say goodbye to people without letting them know you are someone they will soon need to say goodbye to. This may be one of the first lessons these children learn about how to say goodbye in a healthy way. You want to do all you can to make this lesson a positive one.

You should never promise children you will remain their nanny forever. Some children will ask directly. Your answer should be along the lines of, "You will not need me forever, but I will always love you." Children need to know that their relationship with you may not be always same, but they have touched your heart in such a way that you will never forget them.

This moment provides an excellent opportunity to teach children the difference between your role and the role of their parent. Their parent will forever be in their lives. You are there to care for, comfort, and teach them. There will come a time your relationship changes, but the relationship they have with their parent never will.

Once you decide to leave, or the decision is made for you, discuss with the parent what everyone should tell the children. Will you be present when the parent explains your departure to the children? What will your role be in that conversation? You need to respect the parent's wishes on this topic and not confuse the children. Instead, you can set an example of a compassionate goodbye for the children.

Leaving on Good Terms

There is no way to know how the parent will react when you inform her you are leaving. You also have no idea what the parent will say if she lets you go. You can only plan so much, but there are ways you can work to leave on good terms.

Emotions are almost always high during this transition, and the parent might say things that she did not intend to. Have patience with her as she may be grieving the loss of you in the family's life too.

During the transition be respectful of the parent, her wishes, and her role with the children. If the parent says that she wants you to leave without seeing the children, respect that. It is her choice. You may ask to write the children a letter to read later, which will give the parent an opportunity to share it or not.

"In some situations you will not receive a 'thank you' from the parents. They may not be in a place to be able to express their gratitude to you. It is possible that some form of appreciation may be received either at the time or in the future, but, in the end, you need to accept the fact that it may never come at all." Glenda Propst

Chapter 24. Leaving a Job with Grace

How to Do It

You are ready; you have prepared the children as best as you can without giving it away; and now it is time to pull the plug. How do you say what you need to say?

First, you will need to prepare an official letter of resignation. This will provide the reason you are giving notice, the details of how much notice you are giving, and anything else that you need to communicate with your employer. Writing this will help you solidify what you need to say.

After you have written your letter of resignation, you can practice how you will say it. This will also help you work up the nerve to do so.

Telling the parent can be done in a few ways. The professionally preferable way is to do so face to face. Ask the parent to set aside five minutes at the end of the day. Find an activity where you can have the children distracted. They should not be around to hear your conversation with the parent. Have the letter ready in hand. Thank the parent for all she has done, give her positive feedback about her children and how you have loved caring for them, then say the words you have been practicing. Follow it up with something else positive and give her the letter. She may have questions at the time. Be prepared to either answer more questions or give her time to react.

If telling the parent in person is not possible because there is no way to keep the children from hearing it, a phone call is the next best option. You should do this at a time that you are not around the children, and hopefully, the parent is not either. Follow the same steps that you would if talking to her in person. At the end, you can give her a choice to drop off the letter of resignation, or you can email the attachment to her. The letter of resignation should be in a PDF form rather than in the body of an email.

There are very few reasons that you would not be able to at least give your notice over the phone, but if there is some reason, the last option is for you to provide notice or resignation in the body of an email with the official letter of resignation attached. It too would follow the same script a verbal notification would.

Under no circumstances should you ever give notice over a text or other instant message system. Giving notice over text or instant message is an unprofessional way to communicate something so important. If the parent interacts primarily via text or instant message and you are afraid that she will not see the notification via email, you can call or text her to inform her that you sent her an urgent email.

It is critical to give the timeframe of notice that your work agreement states. If you give less than you are required to per your work agreement, then the parent will be less likely to allow you to keep a connection with the children. If you feel up to it, you can even offer more notice than required but leave the final decision up to the parent.

Prepare yourself for the fact that the parent might ask you to leave on the spot, and tell you that she doesn't want you to see the children anymore. A parent can be unpredictable in this situation. Having you say you no longer want to work for her can seem like a personal attack. Even a parent with a good relationship with you may surprise everyone.

What to do if the Parent Lets You Go

You will not always be able to choose the time and place you leave a job. What you do when the parent dismisses you from a position is up to you. Some of it depends on how she follows through on the dismissal and the timeframe she is requesting you leave. For instance, are you being given notice or has she immediately terminated you?

First you need to remain calm. Regardless of what the terms of the release are, you need to stay a professional. Becoming overly emotional will only work to hurt your reputation with the parent, and it may prevent you from being able to say goodbye to the children.

Next you need to ask for the details of why she has fired you. She needs to provide this to you in writing because it will be necessary when you file for unemployment. Insist on this before you leave.

You can ask if there is anything you can do to change the situation if you want to. Otherwise, let the parent know that you respect her decision and that you appreciate the time you have had with her family. Remember that even if you have not always enjoyed the job, you have enjoyed caring for the children. It may be a struggle, but it will send a powerful message to the employer if you say something positive at this time. It shows your professionalism, and, even if she doesn't appreciate it, you know you left the job with grace.

Ask how she would like to handle telling the children, and request a chance to say goodbye. Let her know that while you understand how difficult it will be for the children, you also know that having someone leave their lives without any warning can be a traumatic event that they will take a long time to get over. Let the parent know that you are willing to comply with her stipulations in that goodbye: You will adhere to the words she chooses to use to share the news and you will be sure not to say anything that will cause long-term pain to the children. If she lets you say goodbye, be respectful and follow through on what she asks.

If the parent does not allow you to say goodbye, ask if she would consider reading a letter that you write to the children. If she says no, there is nothing more you can do. You need to let it go.

However, if the employer is receptive, you may want to ask if you can continue to have a relationship with the children in some way. Respect the parent's wishes if she says no to this.

Staying Emotionally Healthy

Leaving a job or being let go from a job is a significant loss. You need to take time to grieve. Make sure that you stay connected in the nanny community. If you have a group locally, members can be a source of great support, but there are many groups worldwide through social media. Glenda's group "Nannies in Transitions" was created for this reason. Reach out to Glenda to join this group.

Conversations with other professional nannies will be valuable to you during this time. There are not many people outside of our industry who understand the pain that you go through when you leave a family.

Try not to wallow in the negative things that have happened, but stay positive. It can be easy to relive the situation over and over again to friends, but it is best not to get caught up in that cycle of anger. Instead, you should get through the pain and move forward. It is OK to review what happened to learn a lesson for yourself, but if you keep stating the same negatives over and over again, you will never move forward. If you need to get all that out, it is best to journal about it rather than spreading negative attitudes about it to friends and family. Spreading negative words can come back to haunt you as you move on to new nanny positions.

Consider what you want to do next. Maybe you need to take time off in between jobs, and perhaps you want to jump back into the hunt, but figure out for yourself what you should do. Maybe you want to take time to learn a new skill, so you improve your marketability. When you do decide it is time to get back to the job search, start with small tasks if you need to so you don't get overwhelmed.

GLENDA PROPST

Glenda Propst is the owner of the blog and Facebook page Nanny Transitions. Her goal is to offer support, information, and resources for nannies who are going through the transition of leaving a family.

Glenda is a founding board member of the International Nanny Association (INA), the 1991 Nanny of the Year, and one of the three founders of the former National Association of Nannies (NAN). She is also a founding team member of the Regarding Nannies Development Team. In 2016 Glenda was awarded the Meritorious Service Award from the INA.

She retired in 2015 after 31 years as a professional nanny, but don't think she is going to disappear. Glenda has a passion for the nanny industry and will continue to work hard to educate and support nannies in every way she can. She is excited about this segment of nanny coaching and is honored to be a part of it.

NannyTransitions.com

Nanny Basics and Beyond

Epilogue

I want to take a minute to thank you for reading this book. It was a labor of love for me. To be able to share all the things that I wish someone had told me before my first job, as well as the tips and tricks I learned from other leaders in the industry, is truly a gift. Twenty-plus years ago when I started working as a nanny, I would have never guessed that I would be helping other nannies learn and grow in the industry.

Thank you to each and every person who I interviewed for this book. I chose you not only because of your wisdom but also the great respect I have for your contribution to the nanny world.

I will leave you with this last piece of advice. Be proud of your place in the industry. Work hard, learn new things, challenge yourself to implement those new lessons, and then share what you have learned with others. We are all united in this industry for the same purpose: to help parents raise happy, healthy, and well-adjusted children so that the next generation of leaders can be that much stronger. Thank you for helping me be a small part of that effort, and I hope that you will choose to share your knowledge with the rest of us. We all have important things we can teach others.

Marcia Hall, September 2018

Nanny Coaching Team

Marcia Hall offers individual Nanny Coaching that can help you gain confidence in communicating with your employers. Individual Nanny Coaching is like having a life coach that centers on your career as a nanny and helps you successfully interact with your current and future employers. It enhances your ability to learn, make changes and achieve the desired goals you have for your career and within the family.

Individual Nanny Coaching can also help you explore your ideal job goals, gain focus on the "must haves," develop skills to land that next great position, identify the frustrations of job "extras," and gain skills on negotiating through them.

Nanny Coaching Team Continuing Education

Not everyone can invest the time or money to attend the many wonderful nanny-related conferences that are available. While Marcia encourages taking advantage of attending these events, she wants to bring you a similar experience that you can access on your own schedule, in your own home, with minimal financial investment.

With Nanny Coaching Team's Build-A-Conference, you can have access to over 35 topics ranging gaining respect from your employers to basic newborn care and safety in the home. Each video is presented by industry leading coaches on a specific topic. Plus we are continuing to build onto the video library with future topics from industry leaders.

Nanny Coaching Team provides you with a private page where all your videos will be housed. You can view them when you like and as many times as you like. Additional video purchases will be added to your private page as you grow your library.

Here is a full list of topics offered:
- The Nanny-Employer Communication System
- Car Seat Safety
- Children's Safety in Public
- Dealing with Conflict
- Dealing with the "Babysitter" Mentality
- Encouraging the Parent-Child Bond
- Gaining Respect from Your Employers
- Getting Paid Legally and Why it Matters

Nanny Coaching Team

- Caring for Yourself while Caring for Others
- How to Choose the Right Job
- An Effective Nanny Share with guest coaches
- How to Navigate the Interview Process
- How to Start the Job Right
- How to Work Professionally in Your Nanny Job
- Leaving a Job with Grace
- Opportunities to Help Your Career
- Safety in the Home
- Technology and Your Nanny Career
- The Annual Review
- The Art of Negotiation and Your Work Agreement
- Being Assertive versus Being Aggressive
- The Dream versus. The Reality
- The Most Effective Resume
- Toxins in Everyday Life
- Understanding Basic Infant Care
- Understanding Children's Food Allergies
- Using Lesson Plans in Your Job
- Worknig With Different Discipline Styles
- Understanding How to Work With Teens
- Understanding Self-Directed Play
- Understanding Your Paystub
- Work Agreements and Why They Matter
- Working as a Nanny/Household Manager
- Working with Divorced or Separated Parents
- Working with Families During Trauma
- Working with High Profile Families
- Working with Multiples
- Working with Special Needs Families

A popular and dynamic presenter, Marcia Hall is available as a keynote speaker and workshop facilitator at industry conferences and events. For more information, you are welcome to contact Marcia through the Nanny Coaching Team website, or at 414-666-1104.

NannyCoachingTeam.com

About Marcia Hall

Marcia Hall has been working with children and families as a professional nanny and an ACPI Coach for Families since 1996. In 2011, she was named the International Nanny Association (INA) Nanny of the Year. For seven years Marcia served the nanny industry on the INA Board of Directors and was elected President of the INA for two years. She currently serves as the INA Executive Director, overseeing the day-to-day operations of the association as well as coordinating the INA Annual Conference.

Marcia founded Nanny Coaching Team in 2014 with a vision to help nannies better understand their unique place within the family. Since then, she has built a library of resources to provide quality continuing education that is available to anyone, anywhere.

Nanny Basics and Beyond

Marcia is an advocate for children in every area of her life, and has served as a children's ministry director, a "Big" with the Big Brothers and Big Sisters program, and as a Girl Scout Troop Leader. Marcia and her husband, Scott, have also been foster parents in Milwaukee, Wisconsin. Though Marcia's full-time job is currently mommy to three amazing children, she will forever be a nanny at heart.

In 2016, Marcia co-authored *Grandpa B's Birch Trees* with her father, Bob Brown. The publication of *Grandpa B's Birch Trees* coincided with Mr. Brown's 70th birthday. *Grandpa B's Birch Trees* is available on Amazon.com. *Nanny Basics and Beyond* is Marcia's second book.

28661311R00211

Made in the USA
Columbia, SC
16 October 2018